NLP
FOR
MANAGERS

NLP
FOR
MANAGERS

**HOW TO ACHIEVE
EXCELLENCE AT WORK**

Dr HARRY ALDER

PIATKUS

First published in 1996 by
Judy Piatkus (Publishers) Ltd of
5 Windmill Street, London W1P 1HF

First paperback edition 1996
Reprinted 1997

The moral right of the author has been asserted

*A catalogue record of this book is available
from the British Library*

ISBN 0 7499 1613 3 (hbk)
ISBN 0 7499 1643 5 (pbk)

Edited by Christopher Long
Designed by Chris Warner
Artwork by Chartwell Illustrators

Data capture and manipulation by Computerset, Harmondsworth
Printed and bound in Great Britain by
Biddles Ltd, Guildford and King's Lynn

To my big sisters
Jean and Mary,
and my little sisters
Daisy and Lynne.

I would like to thank Ian Newton,
NLP Master Trainer with *Stenhouse Consultancy*,
for his help in reviewing the final manuscript.

◄ CONTENTS ►

PART ONE

Background and Principles of NLP

Introduction

NEURO-LINGUISTIC programming – NLP – has been called 'the art and science of personal excellence' and 'the study of subjective experience'. It helps us understand the *difference* between what we do that produces mediocre results or failure, and what we do that brings about success, or excellence. It addresses questions like 'How do I do what I do well?' 'How could I do it better?' 'How can I acquire the skills I admire in others?' Significantly, NLP is not confined to external, observable behaviour, but includes the way we think – the mental processes that control all our experience and achievements. It deals with the whole structure of human experience – in effect what makes people tick – attempting to model the thought processes, feelings and beliefs that result in any behaviour. Especially, it is about communication – with yourself as well as with others.

Although NLP has been around for some years, it has grown rapidly and is now generating a lot of interest in areas such as management and training. Much of the early work in the subject involved modelling 'excellence' in outstanding individuals, and many of its practices have evolved around emulating the 'strategies' which support outstanding behaviour and achievement. As a manager you can use the principles and techniques of NLP to make fundamental and lasting changes in your behaviour, both at work and in your personal life. Based upon what you want to *have* or *be*, you can choose what to *do*. By understanding your own thought processes better, you can learn to take control of habitual, often unconscious behaviour, and start achieving goals which have so far seemed impossible.

Communicating your way to excellence

Communication is central to any manager's effectiveness. It always figures high on the list of criteria for success, and especially when leadership is the topic. Traditional communication theory has often majored on the technicalities of the medium and form of the message, and of late the technology. NLP is more concerned with the variety of perceptions, attitudes and beliefs that are involved. In particular it focuses on the desired outcome, or purpose, of the communication – or of any aspect of behaviour, for that matter – and the extent to which this is achieved. Crucially, NLP is concerned with what *works*, rather than what is the most elegant theory. What exactly do you want to achieve? How will you know your communication has been successful? What will be the 'sensory evidence' – what will you see, hear and feel?

In NLP, success is not measured on the basis of adherence to a script, system, or indeed any effort or other input, but according to whether what you do works. In any interpersonal communication, this means knowing 'where the other person is coming from' – somehow bridging your different perspectives of the world. Understanding how the other person thinks and feels is vital in establishing the rapport upon which successful communication depends. It is a more effective basis for achieving your outcome than the most sophisticated communication system or carefully rehearsed presentation.

Communication is to do with transferring understanding, from one person's mind to someone else's. It starts with you and me rather than 'them'. A communication may be attributed to 'management', 'the shop floor', 'the City', or 'them', but it is all about bridging the gap between individuals, however large a group those individuals represent. Insofar as you or I may want to communicate something, first we need to be clear about what we want to achieve, or we are unlikely to act in a way that makes our meaning clear to the other person.

You may first have to communicate with *yourself*, to know just what you want, and what effect your desired outcome might have on other aspects of your work and life. Then you have to get inside the other person's mind – see things as they see them – so that your communication will make sense to them. If it doesn't, it is unlikely to succeed, however clever the presentation. Successful communication therefore involves subjective thought processes – including feelings and beliefs, yours and the other person's – as well as words and observable behaviour. This is one of the areas of NLP that can turn on its head some conventional management wisdom.

As a manager, how many times have you been amazed at how communication can go badly wrong? How easy it is for the slightest gesture or tone of voice to be taken the wrong way. As well as certain common-sense principles, NLP offers you state of the art communication techniques that will enable you to achieve extraordinary results. And the skills extend to personal effectiveness generally, including managing how you feel – your own state – which may not always directly affect communication with others.

NLP is not a quick fix. The changes that may be involved concern your actual neurological processes – the way you, uniquely, think – and they will be permanent. But the process of change can be very quick indeed – typically minutes rather than hours – even when applied to long-standing habits that in the past might have taken months to put right. Many of the techniques of NLP can be applied on a DIY basis and in day-to-day life, allowing you to experience immediate benefits and build on your success. This book is written with you, the busy manager, in mind, and offers practical techniques you can use immediately in your work, as well as principles you can apply yourself in situations I could not begin to predict.

You can be part of a revolution

I was a manager for about twenty years, in different industries and different kinds of organisation, in the UK and abroad. Although steeped in orthodox communication theory and a willing or unwilling delegate on scores of training courses, my scepticism and disillusionment increased with every year of experience and corporate seniority. In particular, I found that managers, even very senior ones, were often poor communicators, despite formal training and years of being responsible for people. Among the lower echelons, where the real business is carried out, well thought out mission statements were little more than rhetoric, or were even the butt of in-house jokes. The effects, as I saw them, were inestimable. For example, one carefully planned speech by a CEO to reassure staff following layoffs was completely misconstrued by the staff; instead of achieving its aim it engendered fear, mistrust and lower than ever productivity.

In a range of large and small organisations I witnessed all sorts of communication methods – departmental briefings, monthly meetings, training sheep-dips, strategy presentations – adopted in an effort to get messages from the top to the bottom, and sometimes the other way. And again, apart from the wasted expense of the communication, the results often turned out to be counterproductive. True communication – getting real understanding from one mind to another, whatever the means used – hardly happened, at least in a deliberate, conscious sense. Apart from the super-efficient office grapevine, the only instances of effective communication seemed to happen in company 'politics', and during non-work weekend activities in which nondescript managers took on important roles in the community and enjoyed excellent relationships. In other words, communication happened by default, and certainly did not support the corporate mission, or any other obvious organisational purpose.

As a manager you will no doubt have your own communi-cation or personal ineffectiveness horror stories. And maybe, as I was, you are part of the scene – part of the problem. My own experience training hundreds of managers from every corner of commerce and industry has certainly confirmed my earlier doubts as a practising manager. My recent interviews with over 150 top business leaders when I was researching my book *Think Like a Leader* have further confirmed the dearth of communication skills that keep so many managers from becoming leaders – or even effective managers.

NLP is changing all this, and this book will show you how. Communication and personal effectiveness are too important to leave to chance, and are now the subject of well researched processes. Top CEOs who contributed to my earlier books – some of whom are widely acknowledged as masters of commu-nication, as well as outstanding leaders – are taking a special interest in the subject. It makes sense of what has hitherto been considered too intuitive, subjective or unscientific even to discuss professionally. Some large companies now have qualified NLP practitioners on their full-time management training teams.

Management development, including training in communication skills, comes in many guises, of course. Discriminating CEOs are questioning the benefits of much orthodox training, and its purpose in the first place. With delayering and budget slashing, the very role of the manager, in its traditional sense, is being questioned. I and other practising training professionals have been all too aware of gaping holes in the technology of personal effectiveness and communication. From my own vantage point, NLP is set to change this. Some sort of a revolution is going on, and, having come this far in your enquiries, you are likely to be part of it.

You can get what you want

As a manager, you can get from NLP whatever you want. For instance:

- you can become more persuasive;
- you can start to enjoy and excel in communication – whether up-front presentations, or one to one;
- you can start doing amazing things with everyday language to help achieve your objectives;
- you can exchange negative beliefs for more empowering ones;
- you can start to take control of how you feel at important times;
- you can draw on your accumulation of better times from the past, and natural skills, and apply these whenever you want;
- you can draw on the behaviour and skill of *another person* you admire and would like to copy. NLP is the technology of modelling excellence.

In all of this, you will end up knowing yourself better and finding the inner peace – or whatever you might call it – that comes from having greater control and personal freedom, and that will have a beneficial effect on just about everything you do.

It's up to you. In NLP, everything has to be tried, because its success is a matter of practice rather than theory. But you don't have to sell your shirt. Here's a tip which I have found useful: start by considering what you read as not necessarily *true* – just potentially *useful* or beneficial. You can then enjoy the benefits of just one simple exercise or technique before committing yourself to trying another. This way, you have nothing to lose, and any learning is easy and natural.

What you want or what you don't want

Why not have an early taste of some NLP? Do the following very simple exercise. Think of something you do not want to happen – a situation you would prefer to avoid, or an event that would be painful or distasteful. This might involve your job or career, a project you are engaged on, a relationship at work – or whatever. Concentrate on it for a little while. *Experience* the situation – see the sights, hear the sounds, sense the feelings, etc. – just as we do without any prompting when dreading some future event or worrying about things. Write down any words that describe how you feel when imagining your negative outcome.

Now think of something you would *like* to have or happen instead of the negative outcome. Ask yourself, 'If I don't want that, what *do* I actually want?' Then fully experience mentally the positive, pleasurable outcome once again – all the sights, sounds and feelings – just as you might dream of a well-earned holiday in great detail and enjoy it in advance. Again write down any words that describe how you feel.

You probably found that you felt a lot better when thinking about what you wanted than when thinking about what you didn't want. Here are some of the words that typically accompany thoughts of negative outcomes: fear, panic, frustration, sadness, lethargy, helplessness, nervousness, despair, failure, embarrassment, pain, hopelessness, pessimism, annoyance, envy.

Feelings that accompany imagery of positive outcomes are, typically: confidence, pleasure, hope, peace, anticipation, self-worth, power, excitement, thankfulness, optimism, motivation, certainty.

Does how you feel affect what you achieve? Of course it does. And which category of feelings would most support your goals? The answer, although obvious, is one of the most important keys to consistent achievement. And you can create this empowering state *just by thinking*. It is all within your control.

The difference is not just in the mind. Anyone watching you would probably notice the difference in your body posture, breathing and facial expression. There are also internal chemical changes that reflect your outcome imagery and help you on your way to their actual fulfilment. Physiologically, you become what you think. The chances are that in your new, more positive state, you are also more resourceful and motivated, and more likely to actually achieve your outcome. So how you express and imagine your outcome *makes a difference* – perhaps the critical difference between success and failure.

You can try the exercise on other outcomes – just identify things you don't want, and things you would rather have, and note how just thinking about them affects you. This will illustrate the importance of expressing your goals positively, but also how easy it is to change how you feel about something by changing your perspective, and thus how you are likely to actually behave. It also helps to explain how many of the things with which we are preoccupied, because we don't want to happen, actually come about, in a strange, self-fulfilling way. Quite simply we become what we dwell upon in our thoughts. It is as though the brain can only accept the instruction of the imagery we conjure up, overlooking the 'don't' injunction.

You can usually change a negative outcome into a positive one very easily. Sometimes, however, when you are locked into the habit of expressing things negatively, and it seems unnatural to think in a different way, you will need a little ingenuity. And of course setting positive outcomes is *pleasurable*, as we saw from the feelings evoked. This is a nice feature of most NLP processes.

Dwelling on what you don't want is sometimes called worry, and can have bad effects all round, including physical ones. But there is more to it than that. The way the brain processes desires or outcomes is to ignore negatives. 'I don't want to be sick' records as 'sick' on the brain, and 'I don't want to be late for that appointment' is likely to record as 'late'; whereas 'I want to be five minutes early' records 'early' – what you want rather than what you don't want. Hence the wisdom of truisms like the 'self-fulfilling prophecy' or an 'accident waiting to happen'.

One of the tests of a 'well-formed outcome' is simply whether your outcome is expressed in positive terms. Not only does this give the right message to your brain, from where all your behaviour, conscious and unconscious, is processed, but you also feel better – you are in a better state, and more likely to achieve because of your confidence, calmness, enthusiasm, or whatever positive state you access. Negative beliefs and disempowering states, conversely, are self-fulfilling – you will get the very thing you didn't want. But you are free to restate your outcomes, and change how you feel, consciously and quickly.

How can such a simple exercise have any lasting effect, and actually influence what you do and accomplish? Quite simply, a few million of the electro-chemical neural connections in your brain have changed. The neural landscape of your brain has altered, just as when wind and rain changes a natural landscape. You have *experienced* something; you have represented something in the way you choose. Importantly, you have consciously decided what to think and have changed how you feel. You have control. You make the choices. And you create your own future. Amazingly, by changing how you represent what you want, your whole state of mind and behaviour will change. And so inevitably will your future, which is created by what you do. This is a little example of NLP . It's simple and it works.

De-mystifying the name

The name Neuro-Linguistic Programming can be an initial barrier, especially to straight-talking managers who want a minimum of jargon, or of anything sounding too academic or theoretical. The subject, as it happens, is anything but heavily theoretical, and the name does make simple sense.

'**Neuro**' refers to our thinking, or perception – the brain processes and nervous system which form the basis of any behaviour. Specifically, it refers to the neurological processes of sensing – seeing, hearing, feeling, tasting and smelling.

'**Linguistic**' refers to the language patterns which affect our understanding and upon which much communication is based. It is hard to imagine conscious thought without language – how often do we have conversations with ourselves, give ourselves advice, or a telling off?

'**Programming**' refers to the way we can organise and program our thoughts, including feelings and beliefs, to bring about desired changes in behaviour and outcome – much as we program a computer for specific tasks with appropriate software. So much for the title NLP; I will explain any other essential terms as we go along.

Manager-friendly structure

I have structured the book to make sense to managers, rather than to fit NLP. The way the subject has evolved from the early work of its founders, John Grinder and Richard Bandler, in any event does not lend itself to a neat structure for a book covering the subject in full. Although it has a number of foundation principles, sometimes referred to as presuppositions, these tend to pervade every aspect of the subject, rather than form neat compartments in the manner of chapter headings. And apart from 'communication' itself – which certainly represents a large part of management – there are no obvious pigeon-holes that will give a sense of familiarity and accessibility to logically-disposed managers. And as I have said already, definitions of communication may differ.

So I have avoided using an NLP-based structure for the book. After this first part of the book, in which I introduce the subject, outlining its historical background and describing some of its key principles, I relate each subject to important areas of management. Part Two covers goal achievement, which is more or less compulsory in a book aimed at managers. NLP, however, adds new dimensions to the traditional theme of goal-setting. But the planning topic is familiar ground for managers, and it enables me to introduce several aspects of NLP. Part Three covers communication, which I have already referred to as being central both to NLP and also to management. Here you will find dozens of things you can put into practice immediately as a manager, and start to get results. You will also get ideas that can help at a team, department, or company level. Part Four is about personal effectiveness. NLP takes us beyond competence, which has been given a lot of attention in corporate human resources circles, towards excellence and mastery. It identifies the important 'difference that makes the difference'. In terms of personal excellence, NLP has a far wider application than management. It applies to any level in an organisation, and also to sport, family life, and self-development. Part Four reflects a particular aim of the book: to help you as a *manager*, rather than addressing the impersonal world of *management*. NLP applies to you as a total person – personal excellence is never confined to compartments like manager, parent, cook or cricketer. The approach is holistic throughout. Part Five is an NLP approach to problem-solving, including decision-making. The manager has been described as a problem-solver *par excellence*, and you will find plenty here to use in day-to-day problem-solving. The NLP approach, however, is far more creative than traditional problem-solving tools. After reading this part you need never be short of new ideas on even the most intractable problem.

In search of corporate or personal excellence?

The main thrust of NLP is a personal one: excellence, for instance, is addressed more in terms of excellence in people rather than in systems or organisations. So what impact does NLP have on corporate or organisational matters? Although it may not be apparent from many management texts which are biased towards structure and systems, the search for corporate excellence leads inevitably to excellent people – individual people, and especially managers. Once you know what motivates a person, what makes him or her tick, what sort of communication works best, you can begin to be effective at a group, departmental or organisation level. The individual – where NLP puts the emphasis, and where the organisational impact lies – is central to every aspect of organisational behaviour.

There are examples of successful organisations operating with very different structures and systems – for instance, highly centralised or fully devolved. But in each case, in successful organisations, people are communicating, messages are being got across, and individual effectiveness is being harnessed. When vision and values are shared, people know where they are going, so any corporate structure and systems have a head-start. NLP makes its contribution at the people coal face; it does not have much to say about organisational development theory. Its impact, whether in the area of learning, communication, leadership, goal-setting or problem-solving, brings about change at every level. But it happens one person at a time. Human experience is individually crafted, rather than mass-produced. This aspect – the personal impact of NLP – is reflected in each of the main topics, in each part of the book, and also in the practical exercises and suggested applications.

Having set out the structure and basic scope of the book, this introductory chapter will conclude with a brief historical background. I then set out in Chapter 2 a simple four part 'success model' which will form a foundation for much that follows. Then in Chapter 3 I describe some of the main presuppositions upon which NLP is based. But first I will offer some guidance on how you can get the best value from the book, and how you can start applying the techniques in your everyday life and work.

How to get the best out of the book

Have an open mind

Be ready to suspend your judgement, as you may have to discard logical, familiar ways of seeing things. Some of the principles of NLP, especially concerning our very limited and subjective perception of what we insist is 'fact' or 'reality', require a measure of humility and open-mindedness that management science does not usually demand.

Be involved as a total person

NLP is not another package of management techniques, nor is it a grand theory. Its impact is not at a corporate or even systems level, but at the level of the individual human mind – it is all about *you*. Not surprisingly therefore, it affects cherished beliefs and values and disturbs mindsets that are more likely to have been perpetuated than questioned by orthodox management thinking. It does not lend itself to neat classification – like you the engineer, squash player, scapegoat, or manager. NLP helps us to get these different 'parts' working in unison, so that our communication both inside and outside is *congruent*. So don't just wear your manager's hat as you read, be *you*.

Be ready to discard limiting beliefs, and identify unconscious intentions

Everything we do is affected by our beliefs and values – some of which, if we gave them conscious thought, we would decide were neither useful nor rational. For example, a manager may be happy to discharge his responsibility by sending a memo, giving a presentation, calling a meeting or whatever. His belief is 'I've done my job, I can't make it any clearer'. Supporting this may be other beliefs that surface when things don't work out: 'He can't have been paying attention', 'He got the wrong end of the stick' or 'She is just not interested in the facts'. Mixed in with these beliefs there may be an underlying 'outcome' or intention on the part of the manager to impress, or even to mislead, which may involve withholding some information, or shrouding facts in jargon. To add to the communication minefield, this underlying intention might well be unconscious. So there are mixed intentions, resulting in 'mixed messages', or incongruence in the communication. Surprise, surprise, the manager does not achieve what he set out to achieve through the communication.

NLP puts the responsibility for the outcome of a communication on the communicator. In this case the manager is responsible to do what has to be done to bring about the effect he wants on the other people. So, for starters, he needs to be clear of his outcome. If what he then does doesn't work, he needs to do something different rather than blame the other person. Be ready to identify your own beliefs and intentions as you go along, and you can decide whether they are useful or should be discarded.

Give everything a try

First check out mentally that things make sense – imagine situations, see yourself and others, question, visualise. We shall meet some important principles in Chapter 3 which are powerful enough to change your perceptions and behaviour without any system or technique. But you will want to test these for yourself. For instance, it is a precept of NLP that you cannot *not* communicate. You can upset somebody without saying a word, or seemingly without moving a muscle. Have a go at not having any effect on the people around you for an hour or so. You may be quieter than usual, take on a poker face, or cover yourself with a blanket, but you can be sure you will still communicate something to somebody.

The more sensitive you are to the effects of your behaviour, the more you will be able to adjust it to get the outcomes you want. So test out principles and presuppositions, first through mental scenarios, then in real life. See whether they make sense. Then try the actual techniques and practical exercises in the book. The real test of NLP is whether it works, and helps you to achieve what you want to achieve. Ask yourself: 'Is it useful? How can I make it useful?' Although NLP provides plenty of models and structures, the purpose of these is to help you as a person to think and act more effectively. But with all the pragmatism, you will have to do some thinking – perhaps deep thinking – for yourself.

Have patience

Some managers quickly become frustrated if they cannot acquire a skill instantly, especially if there is another person in the group, or a subordinate, who takes it in their stride. This applies particularly to mental rather than physical skills, where different ground rules may apply. But just as when correcting a bad driving habit, it's not the complexity of the skill that is the problem, but rather getting rid of the old habit – or more precisely, allowing the new skill to become as habitual as the others. And habits take time, to acquire and to lose. This is where patience is needed, but it will be well repaid, because once an element of behaviour becomes a habit, you don't need to think about it any more – it's easy. What is three weeks in the context of a lifelong, easy, empowering habit? Strangely, what seems easy usually turns out to be most effective. Put another way, it's actually harder to fail than to succeed.

Keep a few key questions in mind all the way through

- How and when can I apply this?
- How can I benefit from this principle, idea, model or technique?
- How can I *adapt* this to make it more useful?
- Is there a *better* approach?

● What opportunities can I use or create to put this to work?

You may need to deface your book, with words, squiggles or colours, in order to get the best out of it, and not forget any blinding revelations. If you can live with this sacrilege I as author have no problem!

HISTORICAL BACKGROUND

NLP started more than twenty years ago at the University of Santa Cruz in the USA. Its founders were John Grinder, who was an assistant professor of linguistics, and Richard Bandler, who was then a student of psychology and mathematics, having a particular interest in psychotherapy. Their research 'modelled' three psychotherapists who were known internationally to achieve outstanding results in their work: Fritz Perls, an innovative psychotherapist and the founder of Gestalt therapy; Virginia Satir, an outstanding family therapist who has been able to bring about resolutions of seemingly insurmountable relationship problems; and Milton Erickson, the world-famous hypnotherapist, who has been described as the father of modern hypnotherapy.

Grinder and Bandler's aim was to establish the patterns of communication behaviour used by successful therapists, which could then be passed on to others. Rather than a grand theory, the result of their early work was a model which can be used for better communication, faster learning and personal achievement in any field. A further significant contribution to the early work of NLP was made by Gregory Bateson, a British anthropologist who has written widely in the fields of anthropology, psychotherapy, cybernetics and biology. Although there was never any intention to establish a new form of therapy, let alone a field of knowledge on the scale of today, NLP has advanced rapidly, in discovering patterns of success in outstanding people, and, more widely, patterns of excellence in ordinary people in many fields.

Michael O'Brien won the Olympic gold medal in the 1500 metres freestyle swimming by a full six seconds after using simple NLP processes lasting about 1½ hours. This came about after he had experienced serious mental blocks, and when his ultimate goal had been for a bronze or perhaps a silver medal. In widely differing sports, from golf to rifle shooting and basketball, NLP techniques have resulted in extraordinary successes. At a personal level, NLP has been used to give up smoking and other habits. Fast phobia cures, involving many thousands of people, have shown NLP to be something that works, quickly and predictably, but not without opposition from traditional psychotherapy. Managers have overcome lifetime fears of giving stand-up business presentations or speeches at social occasions, or of conducting one-to-one disciplinary interviews. My own research involving leading businesspeople has confirmed that adopting simple mental strategies – perhaps for motivation, decision-making, creativity or communication – can set otherwise ordinary people apart, ultimately positioning them as leaders of vast organisations. But the significance for you and me is that such success strategies can be identified and emulated to bring about equivalent results in whatever area we are working. Because skills are transferable, you don't need to depend on luck or the right parents. You can *learn* the knowledge and skills of personal excellence, just like learning to drive, swim or use a personal computer. That is the essence of NLP.

2

Achieving Outcomes

NLP is based on a simple model of goal achievement. This is not unique to NLP – it is similar to any system, such as domestic central heating, or a robot or missile, in which negative feedback is used to progressively correct the system towards reaching a target. This 'success model' is flexible enough to apply in a corporate, team, or other organisational context as well as personally. Keep in mind the key questions you met in the first chapter (page 14) as you consider the four stages.

Decide what you want

The importance of goal-setting is well established in management, although it is applied principally at a corporate or organisation level. Typically in management seminars I have run, many of the participants have never set personal goals in any recognisable way, even relating to their work. Yet without a goal or outcome, any behaviour is likely to be futile – behaviour can only be successful or worthwhile against some criterion or yardstick. If you don't know where you're going, any road will take you there.

As it happens, at a personal level at least, we have an inbuilt tendency to be goal-oriented. It transpires, for instance, that seminar delegates who have not formalised their goals may nevertheless be strongly goal-oriented; it is simply that their goals are not well expressed, and nor do they operate at a conscious level. A 'non-ambitious' person, for example, who does not want to be involved in the rat race of modern life, but wishes to get off the 'treadmill' or find a simple, relaxed lifestyle, in fact is setting an ambitious goal indeed. Moreover, a stick-in-the-mud at work may set and achieve impressive goals in his or her personal life. An outcome might not seem positive or worthwhile to others, yet can act as just as strong a motivation as any high flyer experiences. The important thing is to accept this inbuilt goal-achieving tendency, and identify those things that are not clear, even though they might operate unconsciously. Whatever you want, *decide* what it is. You can consciously *use* your inbuilt tendency to follow some purpose or intention.

There are important principles which can eliminate the hit-and-miss aspect of goal achievement. In Part Two I describe the NLP criteria to ensure that outcomes are 'well-formed' and 'robust', so that their chances of being fulfilled are increased. For the moment, fixing your goal is simply part of a universal process of achievement. This simple principle puts you well ahead of so many of your peers who lack direction in their work and personal lives.

Do something

The action stage, although always implicit, is not always included in NLP texts. It needs to be stressed for managers, however, even for those managers who are naturally 'activists'. Results in the real world depend upon action, however strong our goal motivation is. There is a difference between dreamers, wishers, and even those with strong resolutions, and real achievers. The action you choose will be whatever you consider is best to achieve your outcome, so the better you define the outcome, the more chance you will have of acting effectively. Initially your behaviour might fail to produce the outcome, just as a missile when first launched may veer from the direction of the target. But it is likely to follow the right general direction, which will enable the feedback system, upon which eventual success depends, to operate. Similarly, we have to set off in some direction or other – we have to *act*.

A major system at work may be in need of change – it is not working. You may not know just what the replacement system will be but the chances are you will have some ideas. For example, it may have to be computer-based. It may have to serve another department or section, so other interests are involved. It may have to be flexible enough to accommodate changes in a couple of years if the nature of the business changes, and so on. The point is, you have a general direction in which to go – gathering information, talking to people, asking for comments from the main users, getting technical opinions say about software, checking on what happens in other companies, and so on. More than likely, your first ideas will change out of all recognition, but this is part of the process of making things happen, and of eventually getting what you want. This inevitably means that 'mistakes' will be made, if that is how you want to describe them, and this is an important part of any manager's job. Doing something – even making the first telephone call – is part of the essential process of learning.

Studies of top achievers invariably show that they are decisive and willing to act in situations when others just talk and plan. They also seem ready to make mistakes in the pursuit of goals further ahead. 'Mistakes' have to be accepted as just part of the positive process in which the more we act, the more feedback we will have upon which our direction and ultimate success depend. Sound advice might be 'Never set a goal without also taking the first action to bring it about.' This might mean a simple telephone call, a memo, or a request for information, but it will give you momentum and help commitment. The simple message is *do something*.

Notice what happens

Noticing what happens provides the necessary feedback that establishes the extent to which we are off target – did what I expected to happen actually happen? How far was I off target? The so-called TOTE model – Test, Operate, Test, Exit – which you may have met before, comes into play. We test to see whether we are getting nearer to our target or goal, and if not we *operate* – do what we think will bring us nearer to our goal. We might have to test and operate many times before we eventually reach our target, at which point we exit.

An important aspect of NLP is 'sensory acuity', our ability to notice, by seeing, hearing and feeling, the result of any behaviour. The better our observation, the better we will be able to decide upon a different behaviour that will bring us nearer to our goal. We need to pay attention and literally use our senses.

In making enquiries about a replacement system in your office, you may take the opportunity to visit another organisation which is doing roughly what you intend. You may also read articles that cover some part of what you are after, and from which new ideas will emerge. Then you might bounce what you have seen, heard and felt off a colleague one evening. In this mass of sights, sounds and feelings there will be some helpful information which will take you nearer to your own goal. The crucial insight might be a sentence you read, a passing comment from your colleague, something you saw on a visit to another organisation, or a feeling you had, waking up the following morning, that seemed to indicate a certain direction. Obviously the wider you spread your net of enquiry, the potentially richer will be your own understanding of the possibilities. But, similarly, the more you are able to notice – which might mean better listening, being more visually observant, and perhaps noticing how you feel – the more chance you will have of bridging the gap between where you are and where you want to be – first in the mind, and then in reality.

Fortunately, as well as having an inbuilt goal-setting tendency, we are also equipped with extraordinary sensory powers, although to be effective we need to be confident of them and use them to the full. Personal excellence is mainly to do with using these facilities, rather than relying on some genetic advantage or luck. As with any natural ability, such as in sport or art and crafts, our skill increases with practice and application. Later, I will describe techniques to develop your sensory acuity. This stage has its corporate counterpart in the process of monitoring against plans and budgets – exceptions reporting – that is a large part of the manager's role. It only makes sense if the outcome is specific and observable.

Be flexible

You then have to be prepared to change what you are doing in response to what you notice, again with an eye on your outcome. This is often the sticking point, especially for managers and other professionals whose training does not promote creativity. Radically different approaches are often needed. The standard wisdom is 'try, try and try again'; the

NLP approach is 'If at first you don't succeed, try something different' – anything other than the behaviour which your experience shows guarantees you will miss your goal. Or, put another way, 'If you always do what you've always done, you'll always get what you've always got. If what you are doing is not working, do something different.'

Faced with an impasse, managers typically do more of the same thing. If a promotional mailshot brings in a 1 per cent response, the tendency, to increase sales, is to increase the mailshot – in effect to do more of the same thing. This behaviour is reinforced by norms, both for the organisation and the industry, in terms of hit rates. Now by changing the message, or the medium, or the market focus, there is no guarantee that you will carry on getting a 1 per cent response rate. But it is almost certain that you will get a *different* response – different actions tend to bring different results. And you will never know which is the best action until you try it.

The radical changes in selling insurance and banking services directly by telephone illustrate how dramatic the effect of doing something different can be – in some cases changing a whole industry. Any public relations consultant will argue that by doing something very differently it is possible to bring about business that millions of pounds of advertising budget, or promotional mailshotting, could not have achieved. 'Different' does not have to be sensational. Thinking genuinely in terms of the customer, rather than as a supplier – however much a departure this might be from past practice – is usually no more than common sense. Of course, all this, at the very least, means change. Opening a bank branch – or for that matter a shop – at times that are convenient to the customer, rather than to the proprietor, would at one time have been thought of as preposterous. But flexibility and willingness to change are part of the success cycle, whatever change may be involved.

Change may mean a different attitude, and in some cases will require different skills. There are techniques for creative problem-solving, which I have included in Part Five. In particular, it impinges on how we *perceive* our behaviour, and interpret its outcomes, especially in terms of so-called failure. It also involves personal risk-taking which many managers are averse to. But we will not know success or failure unless we are ready to change what we do.

Fear of failure, besides restricting action generally, applies particularly when we have to move out of our zone of familiarity and comfort. Managers often prefer a rule book or some other safe organisational basis for their actions. Most of us are slow to change unless a logical, well-charted path is laid out for us. These innate attitudes involve the very basis of our thought structure, which NLP addresses head-on. They can be changed to accommodate present outcomes and choices.

Figure 1 illustrates this four-stage model, which is dynamic and forms a cycle:

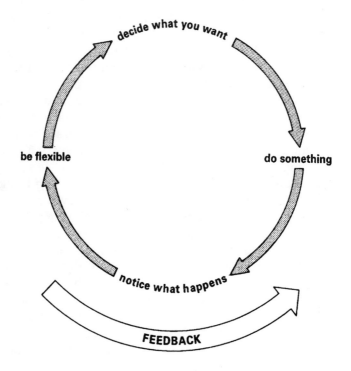

FIGURE 1 The four-stage success cycle

Apart from the constant, and by nature subjective, perceptions involved, our desires can change. In practice, we amend or abandon previously important outcomes as we go along. We 'adjust our sights', becoming more realistic or seeking a bigger challenge, or simply change our mind. So we return in the cycle to deciding what we want, restating our goals, and moving towards them. The NLP principles set out in Chapter 3 are complementary to this simple and universal 'success model', and will help you to apply it more consciously and effectively.

3

Principles and Presuppositions

A NUMBER of ideas, sometimes referred to as presupposi-tions, have been formulated over time as NLP has evolved. Some of these, having stood the test of time and acceptability among students and practitioners of NLP, now form the underlying principles. Unlike the laws of physical science or mathematics, these presuppositions are used more as philo-sophical guides than hard, unbendable rules. Rather than being revered as absolute truth, they are seen as 'useful'. Even more so than in other social sciences, this reflects the highly subjective and unpredictable nature of what is being studied – human thought and behaviour. However, these presupposi-tions, when applied in a wide range of practical situations, do tend to represent a kind of instinctive wisdom – or simple common sense.

People work perfectly

As goal-achieving, purposeful systems, we are remarkably effective. Thus, when we do the same things again and again, we tend to bring about the same sort of results. The *system* works quite well – in fact perfectly. Or if negative intentions are somehow allowed to get into our program, they are efficiently fulfilled – the things we dwell upon in the form of fears and worries have a tendency to become reality. Specific thoughts, actions and feelings consistently produce specific results. Again, although we may input 'garbage', or our intentions may be misguided, the programs that transform our thoughts and beliefs into reality are strangely effective. Of course we often 'program' the wrong thoughts and beliefs into what we do, and are unhappy with the results.

It is often the case that when you dwell on particular fears or situations that are worrying to you, you fall off the bike, have a dry mouth when you make a speech, turn up late for an appointment, or whatever. Your conscious or unconscious intentions are slavishly obeyed to become real behaviour and events. Conversely, it follows that, by simply *changing* how we think about something, how we perceive it, our behaviour will change and we can be confident of a satisfactory outcome. Whether by design or default, the system works. As we have seen already, our flexibility in changing is the secret to success. The system works – we just need to understand and trust it. Once we know how to create and maintain our inner thoughts and feelings, we can begin to direct our total neuro-physiological system to getting what we consciously want.

The successful practice of NLP will normally depend upon the acceptance of this and the following underlying principles; thus a measure of faith is required, at least at first.

The meaning of communication is the response it produces

The success of a communication depends on whether it achieves the outcome intended. The purpose of communication, like any behaviour, is to bring about an outcome, such as to pass on information, to warn, entertain, encourage, or whatever. Whatever form the communication takes in terms of the message or medium, and whatever the sophistication of the 'input' behaviour, unless it fulfils the desired outcome it is ineffective. Conversely, a 'communication' that fulfils its outcome – even without words, or a recognisable message – is effective.

This places a lot of the onus on the communicator rather than the communicatee. Being convinced that you 'spelt it out clearly' will not ensure the outcome you intended – you may have to find a different way to get your message across. NLP identifies and measures success on the basis of the *outputs*, rather than the *inputs* of the communication. A speech by the managing director that produces scepticism and anger is ineffective if its intention was to reassure staff and raise morale

– however polished the audio visual aids, and however carefully chosen the words. Similarly, if you are giving someone a serious warning and they take it humorously or light-heartedly, you have failed in your communication. Blaming their attitude, or even intelligence, will not make your communication any more successful.

A CEO whom I once interviewed came across as highly creative and in favour of empowering his people to make their own creative contributions to the company. Whether this was true or not, if it was his intention to communicate this to me, he succeeded. Later discussions with people at a lower level in the company made it clear, however, that he was perceived as quite autocratic, and in practice did not allow freedom of ideas. If it was his intention to communicate his wish for a blame free, creative culture to his immediate team and middle managers, he seems to have failed. The important point here is that you cannot just rely on the words you say. Communication is much more than that, and there has to be belief in what you are saying, which requires congruency in your behaviour. But even a seemingly congruent communication does not happen in isolation. You have to live with your past communications and perceptions of your values. Any parent knows the importance of consistency in getting across a message to a child; yet there are plenty of managers, and managing directors, who could benefit from the principle.

This principle highlights the importance of the non-verbal, and any less overt aspects of the overall process. Feelings and attitudes, for instance, on the part of both people, may be involved in the transfer of understanding from one human brain to another. If you believe that bosses are only out for what they can get, or that they just think in the short term, your understanding of any communication from them is likely to be filtered accordingly. Conversely, if you greatly admire your charismatic chairman, you are likely to take just about anything he says in a favourable light. And this works in two ways – how *you* communicate with your bosses will also be affected by your attitudes and beliefs. So in order to achieve what you want by a communication, as well as sorting out your intentions (which may, as in the above examples, be distorted by your attitude) you may have to be prepared to reconsider your own map of the situation. Our *perceptions*, or the very structure of how we think, may have to change in order to bring about a desired outcome.

You cannot not communicate

We have already met this presupposition. We are all communicating all the time, mostly non-verbally. The faintest sigh or smile, even the angle of your body, are all communication, whatever your conscious intention. That is, somebody is likely to read something from them. Even our inner thoughts – in effect our internal communications – are often passed on to others, through our posture, body movements, voice tone or eye movements. This is linked with the previous presupposition, in that the responses of others – sometimes unexpected ones – are evidence of the communication. Knowing the effect of different forms of communication is a powerful tool for any manager. Understanding that we are always communicating adds an extra dimension of responsibility.

The map is not the territory

We each perceive the world uniquely, as though in possession of an individual map of the real world, one we have charted ourselves. To start with we, as human beings, are individually only able to access a tiny part of the energy waves around us in the form of sights (light waves), sounds and other sensual stimuli. So our understanding is based on a sample, or tiny sensory window on the real world. We are also each unique in our collection of past experiences, and the attitudes and beliefs these have resulted in. We tend to filter experience to 'fit' our perceptions and beliefs. Millions of electro-chemical synaptic brain connections, rather than what we perceive with our eyes and ears, become the 'understanding' that forms our individual map of the world. But none of our maps is the 'territory' of reality – it cannot be.

True communication, therefore, must attempt to understand other people's perceptual maps. By recognising differences, we become aware of the richness and variety of human experience. By sharing other maps and adjusting our own from time to time, rapport increases and communication is made more effective. The map analogy can be humbling, and should make us think again about what is 'fact'. It explains why the same situation or behaviour can be viewed by different people in very different ways. Even our own memories can become far removed from reality, as they are filtered by our present experience and perceptions each time we recall them. NLP offers a model that helps us to understand the structure of these mental maps, enabling us to share otherwise subjective, incommunicable experiences. Bridging these maps is the essence of communication.

Think of all this in terms of the people you communicate with regularly – bosses, fellow managers, your own staff, and those you have no line responsibility for. How might their maps differ from yours? And how might such an under-standing affect how you communicate, and the effectiveness of your communication? Does an accountant, or an engineer, or a marketing professional have different perspectives? Does a person who has travelled a lot, or had many jobs, see things differently? And what about a person who is a lot older or younger than you? You may be surprised at how a simple awareness of these differences helps in creating rapport and effective communication. 'If I were her, what would it take to convince me? What would be important? How would I feel?' In thinking like this, your own map is enriched, longer-term rapport is established, and future communication is made more effective.

Experience has a structure

All our thoughts and memories have a pattern to them. The brain attempts to classify or categorise all the sensory data it receives through the eyes, ears and other sensory 'receptors'. This is how we can make meaning of such an enormous mass of data. But for each individual any preference to use one modality (say, to think in pictures) more than another will tend to form a pattern or structure of thought – regardless of the content of the thought. In addition, the characteristics or submodalities of these inner representations, such as the brightness of the picture or loudness of the sound, will also form a structure. So, for example, different unhappy memories might well have a similar structure, which of course produces the common feature of unhappiness. The sequence, or syntax, of thoughts is also part of the structure of experience, and one person might be motivated initially by visual images, followed perhaps by good feelings, while another person may be triggered by internal dialogue, or self-talk, which may be followed by a visual or any other representation. So a motivation strategy – say for getting out of bed, or starting a job you do not want to do (but want to have done) – will have a structure for each person. When we change this pattern, we change the meaning of the thoughts, our state, and probably also our subsequent behaviour. By simply 'seeing something in a different light', our thought structure changes, and we create new experience.

We already have all the resources we need

All our skills and achievements start off in the mind – as thoughts, dreams, pictures of what might be. These building blocks of our mental and physical resources are available to us all. We are able to change how we feel, and to apply ourselves to whatever we want to accomplish. The skills and abilities we use to obtain external resources (like money) – to achieve what we want – stem from these inner resources. You might put it in this way: 'If anyone can, I can'.

We always make the best choices available to us

We each have a lifetime of experience upon which to draw when making choices or decisions. However our success is rated by others, we tend to make the best choices given our own experience, which has served us well to date to some degree at least. Until we are aware of new options, we will continue to make the best choices we can. One of the other presuppositions is that it is better to have plenty of choices, and NLP offers ways of creating them. After all, we can always choose how we feel about something, or our attitude, even if we cannot change external realities.

There is no failure – only feedback

If you miss the golf ball completely, you have not failed – you have simply experienced what it is like to miss a golf ball. A thousand other 'hit and miss' experiences will help you to achieve what you finally want over on the green. If you mess up a short speech, you have not 'failed'. You have learned what to do to produce a certain outcome – in this case not the one you wanted – and so what not to do if you want a different result. As this or any sort of skill depends upon practice and sensitivity, failure does not really come into it. So-called 'failure' is the only way to excellence. It is all part of the learning process.

If you completely blow a speech, or if a meeting you are chairing crumples into anarchy, what three things will you do differently next time? And how soon will you get a chance to try them? How grateful are today's top managers for experiencing the early disasters they can recount in profusion? When does failure become a vital learning stepping stone? In fact the perception of 'failure', even in a normal process of acquiring a new skill, can be counterproductive. Through NLP our perceptions, or attitudes, are something we can control if we wish to.

Every behaviour has a positive intention

It is hard for us to understand any positive reason for behaviour which we think is wrong or misguided. But this is failure to understand the different perceptual maps by which others operate. If something fits our map of what is right or sensible, the behaviour is 'positive', and has meaning. It would be rare indeed for a terrorist or common criminal not to express a reason for his behaviour that made positive sense to him.

In all sorts of cases, apparently strange behaviour turns out to reveal some intention of which we were not aware at the time. A desire for attention or recognition, for example, although more obvious in children, who may do just about anything to gain attention, is often the cause of so-called unexplained behaviour. Few people would include any sort of sickness in their declared goals, but the behaviour of millions may be influenced by the direct or indirect outcomes of behaviour associated with an ailment. In some cases the only way a lonely person can get a long-desired visit is by pursuing a 'strategy' of being sick, or perhaps having an accident – in fact any behaviour that brings about their positive, although usually unstated and maybe unrecognised real intention.

Because some of our 'intentions' are and remain below our consciousness, this presupposition can only be treated as 'useful' – we need not waste time arguing its application to the inevitable extreme examples of unaccountable behaviour. But the presupposition can be applied in various ways, not least in changing how we feel about somebody else's behaviour. And the presupposition may apply to us as well as to others. Sometimes it is far from obvious why we pursue certain habitual behaviours we are not happy with, and which make no logical sense. Identifying our own intentions, and those of others, is part of understanding our respective maps of reality, and is the essence of successful communication. Some first line managers fail because they still want to identify as 'one of the lads', and are unhappy with the image of management. Although consciously they may discount these thoughts in pursuing their career, the underlying intention (to remain popular, to be accepted, etc.) does its job, and effectively scuppers their conscious goals. A similar phenomenon occurs when a highly effective number two takes on the top position, and the new responsibilities (like making the Christmas party speech, dealing with the main board, or handling the press) that go with it. This comes right down to your values and personal identity, and often constitutes the difference between a manager and a leader. The point here is to know what you want, including underlying intentions which, whilst positive or 'reasonable' in themselves ('to be one of the girls', 'not to be made to look a fool', 'not to be seen to be inadequate', 'to have a simple life') may be in conflict with other, more conscious career or personal intentions.

The mind and body are part of the same system

Our thoughts instantly affect our physiology – muscle tension, breathing, how we feel, and much more – and all these in turn affect our thoughts. When we change either, we change the other. Neither part of us can work independently. Our unconscious mind, of course, can have an effect on our body, even when we are not consciously aware of what is going on. The great majority of our 'thoughts' are of the unconscious variety, and these play a big part, as far as NLP is concerned, in our effectiveness. So we have two routes to change: through our physiology and behaviour, and also through how we think. Recognising and using both routes adds a bonus synergy to our effectiveness.

Managers react differently to these principles. You may be sceptical, using your logical, enquiring mind to think of 'exceptions', or perhaps discounting the notion of an intention that operates below the conscious level. Some managers will not accept that they do not have a personal monopoly on 'reality'. The flexibility of thinking required by NLP is also part of its success, as we saw in the success model earlier. The practical nature of the subject, however, means that you can try out the principles and techniques and see for yourself whether they work. Then you in turn – and this is also part of the success of NLP – can make your own contribution to the evolving search for communication mastery and personal excellence.

◄ PART TWO ►

Achieving Outcomes

4

The Technology of Goal Achievement

PLANNING and goal-setting are probably always high on your agenda. Most of us look on planning as an investment – the time and trouble it takes is usually well repaid. Half a minute's thought about what you want to get from a telephone call or a short personal meeting, and how you can best achieve it, is likely to increase your effectiveness. Your hit-rate of getting the results you set out for could increase several times over. Into the bargain you will save on telephone costs and use less precious time. In the case of larger tasks and projects, good planning may mean not just using less time, money and other resources, but the difference between success and failure. So it obviously helps to get your goals written down, or, in the case of an organisation, formalised in some way. But there's a lot more to it than that, and it is in this area that NLP provides powerful technology.

The four-stage success cycle illustrated in Chapter 2 makes clear the importance of setting outcomes. This is central to NLP, which identifies the criteria needed for a 'well-formed outcome'. These are common-sense tests you can apply to any goal or objective. NLP also incorporates powerful techniques involving our inner 'representation systems' – seeing, hearing, feeling – sometimes just referred to as visualisation, which harness our natural neurological faculty to achieve goals. This involves highly subjective processes, which some managers are slow to understand and trust. So both sides of the brain are brought into play – the logical, organised left side, which we associate with conventional planning and organising; and the creative, imaginative, subjective right side, which is also associated with the unconscious mind.

This part of the book covers the important management topics of planning and goal-achievement. In this chapter I introduce goal achievement from different viewpoints, using different models. Each of these can be applied to any of your goals, whether personal or business. In Chapter 5 I describe the criteria NLP applies to outcomes, and in Chapter 6, the principles and techniques of using visualisation, or inner 'representations' to bring about outcomes and create the future you want.

This is the technology, or 'how to', of getting what you want as a manager, whether personally or within a group or organisation. To get the most out of this part of the book, why not make out a list of things you want – big or small, long-term or short-term, betting certainties or just wishes. I will not split hairs on the definition of a goal – I just mean something you want to have or to happen. Then you can apply each principle or technique in a practical, beneficial way as you go through.

GETTING TO A DESIRED STATE

From the first viewpoint the goal achievement 'problem' is to get from one state (where you are now) to another state (where you want to be). Here the goal is invariably a package, including how you feel, or the state you are in, as well as what you want to achieve in a physical or material sense. For example, in producing that important report on time you probably want to feel you have done a good job and to know that it will be appreciated and perhaps acted upon. Rather than just a physical document, your goal might really be a further outcome – such as the implementation of a policy, or agreement to an investment proposal – and the personal satisfaction its achievement will bring you.

Unconscious intentions

These related or implicit goals and intentions may not be stated, or even consciously set, and in any event they will not be formally identified. But they will affect your success hit rate if they are brought into the package, so the sooner and more clearly you identify just what you want the better.

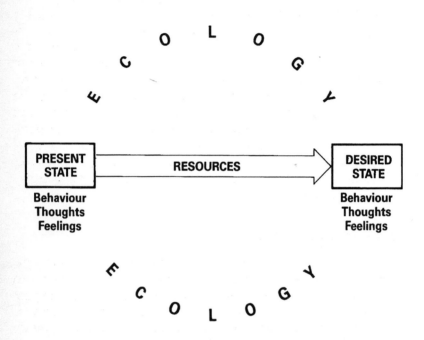

FIGURE 2 Getting to a desired state

Figure 2 illustrates this way of looking at achieving your goals. Both 'states' may involve resources (tangible ones like money and property, or intangible ones like skills and knowledge); behaviour (you may want to act differently); thoughts and feelings. Achieving your outcome means making the journey from A to B, marshalling whatever resources you need, and all this within the framework of other goals and constraints. This framework, or environment, is known in NLP as the 'ecology' of your outcome. Just as everything in the natural environment is linked, so are all our other outcomes, as well as those of others we care about, and we cannot act in isolation from these other outcomes.

Bridging the goal gap

To achieve your goal, you have to bridge the gap. Having decided clearly where you want to get to, that *process* becomes your preoccupation. The many smaller outcomes along the 'journey' – acquiring resources, gaining skills perhaps, or changing how you feel – will seem far less formidable than the eventual goal. Nevertheless, the overall process is likely to involve change, in your behaviour, thoughts and feelings. And it may require motivation and energy. The desired state has to be something you really want, otherwise it is unlikely you will make the journey, crossing whatever hurdles are in your path, to get where you want to be. So think about any of the goals you have listed in these terms. What knowledge, resources, skills and states of mind do you need to get from where you are to where you want to be?

Empowering feelings

The term 'state' is a broad one, and might well include your actual 'state of mind'. Important personal goals often tend to be more to do with our state of mind than objective or tangible factors, and these feelings are what empower us to succeed. For example, while an immediate or short-term goal might be to have a new car, get a salary increase, or go on safari, the goal package will involve how we *feel* about these things, and the pleasure we perceive. Our 'higher-level' goals might be more to do with being financially secure, being fulfilled, or simply being happy. And these are states of mind – one person might be happy in a situation that makes another person sad, and vice versa.

So, unlike companies and other organisations, which do not have feelings – or, for that matter, purposes and outcomes, other than through their people – your change of state journey may take you into subjective territory, and you may have to call on inner resources (like how you feel or what you believe) to help you on the way. The good news is that you can take control of these thoughts and feelings, and channel them towards specific outcomes.

A learnt process

This model involves change, which can be very uncomfortable. Change not just of outward behaviour, but at the level of attitude and perhaps beliefs – what you believe about yourself and others, for instance. In fact change involves each of the stages in the success cycle we met earlier:

- Decide what you want;
- Do something;
- Notice what happens;
- Be flexible.

It concerns you as an individual and how you perceive things. However, it is a *learnt* process, and one which can be repeated whatever the actual goal, to give consistency and predictability to goal achievement. 'High achievers' do not have a special sort of grey matter in their brains. They have simply learnt the process of achieving their outcomes – usually by attempting and apparently failing many more times than less successful people. So learn to welcome change, because change is what creates different, more desirable futures.

The change environment

The framework or environment in which change takes place is the ecology. This comprises the factors that might influence your getting from one state to another, including your other outcomes, and the outcomes of other people, that might have a conscious or subconscious effect on what you do and whether you succeed. A career goal, for example, while commendable in isolation, might play havoc with social goals and family relationships. 'Ecology' is an important NLP topic we shall meet later in this part of the book.

REACHING YOUR TARGET WITHOUT TRYING TOO HARD

Another angle on goal-setting and achievement involves the way the human neurophysiological 'system' responds, sometimes unconsciously, to an internal goal. Here, again, it is not just what you do consciously to achieve your goal – sometimes the harder we try the more we seem to miss the target – but trusting your innate ability to pursue a clearly imagined outcome. In this case it is not so much that your goals or intentions are unconscious, but that, given a clear goal, you *do* things automatically (without thinking, in a conscious sense) that help you reach your goal. The trick is to make the goal so real internally that one way or another you will achieve it. We see plenty of examples of people who fit this model. Their goal, dream or ambition is so clear and certain that, somehow or other, you know they will get what they are after. And more often than not they do, though very different styles and approaches may be adopted from person to person.

Goal-achieving systems

This approach to goal achieving can be described as *cybernetic*. A cybernetic system is one which continuously corrects itself on the basis of negative feedback – how far it is off-target – until the programmed target is reached. A missile, robot, or ordinary central heating system are examples. 'Management by exception', in which only differences from plan are highlighted for corrective action, is a management variant.

The cybernetic model of goal achievement involves a clear target or outcome, a feedback mechanism that tells when you are off the mark, and some ability to correct course progressively until you eventually hit the target. We have already met it in the four-part success cycle in Part One. In the case of the domestic heating example, you set the thermostat target at 70 degrees or whatever, the system detects when it is off target, and the boiler responds, getting you back to where you want to be. All sorts of natural and industrial systems follow the same pattern.

The human cybernetic system

The human brain and nervous system offer the best example of a cybernetic system. It is staggeringly sophisticated, most obviously in the way our vital 'life goals', such as breathing and pulse rate, are regulated without a moment's conscious thought. In these examples the system is inbuilt, which is fortunate in the case of our main body functions which are regulated with great precision. If your temperature drops from its pre-set target you automatically shiver to generate the heat to get back to where your temperature should be. If you get too hot, fluid flows as sweat just like a car cooling system. It is all automatic.

For more complex activities (although those I have mentioned are themselves pretty sophisticated) the same automatic system is at work. The only difference is that, unlike pulse and breathing rates, you can *consciously* set goals – to fasten your laces, eat a sausage, compete in a race, or meet the monthly sales target. Far less well understood is our inbuilt ability to achieve conscious goals by harnessing the unconscious, which is where NLP can help. This approach means getting your outcome well fixed internally and trusting your automatic pilot to progressively steer you around the many obstacles encountered along the journey.

Harnessing natural faculties

The magic of goal achievement happens when we harness these cybernetic faculties, working at an unconscious level, rather than trying consciously. We excel in situations when the *system* can do it best. Once the system is up and running, you can clean your teeth, drive a car, make a golf swing, manage a project, run a department or carry out any other skilled activity with amazing unconscious competence. In fact, the more you think about these habitual activities, the worse you get. Try driving normally with an expert instructor sitting next to you, or fastening your tie when being watched by a group of people.

There is always a first time, of course, to change gear or do a hill start, give a speech, chair a meeting, present a report to the big boss, or fire somebody. But by applying the four-part success cycle, and trusting your natural ability to learn and achieve, the learning curve can be very steep in this early skill-acquiring phase. We certainly need not struggle in mediocrity time after time, year in and year out. Good habits can be acquired as easily as bad ones, and building up a wide portfolio of such unconscious skills is what personal excellence is all about.

Unconscious competence

The idea of unconscious competence keeps recurring in NLP, and is one of the keys to personal effectiveness. Ask your friends and family what you are really good at. The chances are you might not have thought of the skills or talents they mention as being particularly special, and nor will you be able to explain exactly how you accomplish them. The best things we achieve we do without consciously trying; this certainly applies to skills and talents we think of as natural. Your overall objective then should be to get as many of your goals you listed into this 'without thinking' category. You can probably think of colleagues who already take such outcomes in their stride – giving an impromptu speech, managing their time, handling difficult people, or whatever. And you can be sure that their brain matter is not special. It's just that they have somehow relegated these tasks and skills to the level of unconscious competence, as you have done in other areas of life. NLP enables us to model such excellence, transferring the unconscious thinking strategies that account for remarkable success.

YOUR HIERARCHY OF GOALS

The third way to look on goals is as a hierarchy, with lower-level, short-term goals contributing to bigger ones. This is a familiar model in organisations, in which the mission at the top of the goal hierarchy is supported by corporate, divisional and functional goals to form a coherent operating plan. Departmental plans will in turn form the consolidating goal of individual manager's objectives. Individual job descriptions will in turn constitute specific daily tasks and will form the bottom of the hierarchy. Figure 3 (overleaf) illustrates a typical hierarchy.

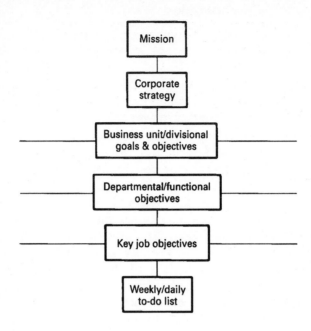

FIGURE 3 Hierarchy of organisational objectives

Your personal mission

Your personal goals will also form a hierarchy. High up there might appear 'be more content' and down below perhaps 'get the fax off to Milan before five o'clock'. Somewhere in between might appear 'get a good half-year appraisal score'. Low-level goals contribute to intermediate ones, which you hope will in turn bring about your higher-level aims. These, together, represent where your holistic intentions lie, just as your company's goals and objectives eventually form a single, coherent business plan.

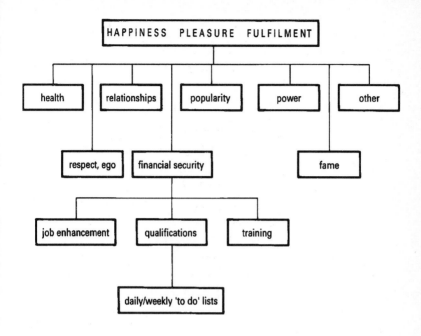

FIGURE 4 Hierarchy of personal goals

A personal 'mission' to 'be happy' will need to be supported by a whole hierarchy of goals; at the next level, perhaps 'to be financially secure'; then to 'get area manager post'; then maybe to get a certain qualification, and so on down to tasks on today's 'to do' list which will hopefully contribute to successive higher-level goals.

Goals that relate to immediate behaviour tend to be specific, although higher, less tangible ones may also be achieved as a consequence. By establishing your own hierarchy, you will begin to see whether the day-to-day tasks on which you spend time and energy are taking you where you actually want to go in the medium and longer term. The exercise is invaluable as a way to get more out of the limited time you have.

Mixing work and personal goals

Work and personal goals will inevitably overlap, and you will have to integrate them into a single hierarchy. Treating them separately is a recipe for failure – certainly in one area, and probably in both. Work goals may conflict with non-work commitments, and managing your total time involves every part of your life. To be effective, your overall goals need to be congruent, both with other goals at the same level, and in contributing to more important, perhaps longer-term, higher-level goals you have identified, and as between work, social, domestic and personal interests.

LIFE CONTENT

The fourth way to think about goals and planning concerns just that - the way we *think* about them. Each of us structures our thoughts differently; we have different preferences about how we behave, and different things are important to us. In NLP jargon we have different 'perceptual maps'. One person is concerned with gaining knowledge, another with getting involved in hands-on action, and another puts the material evidence of achieving a goal first. The so-called Life Content model I will describe later helps us to understand these funda-mental personal differences, and how they affect our goal-setting and achievement.

Goals can usually be categorised into five main types:

- having or getting
- doing
- knowing
- relating
- being

For example to get a new job or house; to do a course at night school; to learn some new subject (knowing); to be respected or admired by other people (relating); to be secure, or content. The way we express our goals often reflects a Life Content disposition. *Doing* a computer course, *knowing* how to program, *getting* the qualification, *joining* the group (relating), and *being* happy in what you are doing may be linked up, but the way you think about and express your goals reveals which ones are important, and the way you will behave to achieve your higher-level goals.

Goal-achieving strategies

You should be able to place your own goals, instinctively listed, into these categories and learn something about your own Life Content strategy. For example, 'I want to get on well with my boss' is a relating outcome. 'I need to understand the new product range' is in the knowing category. 'I want to do a post-graduate course in sociology' or 'I want to spend more time with my children' are concerned with doing, while 'I'd like a diploma in sociology' may indicate a having or getting tendency, as would 'I want my own office'. A 'being' goal might be 'I'd like to be a director' or 'I'd like to be a better parent'. You can see how apparently similar goals are approached in different ways, and involve different sensory evidence of achievement. These are examples of 'strategies', and will be covered in a different context in Part Four. At this stage, the Life Content model allows you to think about your outcomes in a different way. You might want to amend them, perhaps emphasising *knowing* more than *getting*, or *being* rather than *doing*, so that your goals become more compelling and are thus more likely to be achieved. If your ambition is to write a book, for instance, which is most compelling? 'I want to write a book'; 'I want to get a book published'; or 'I want to be an author'. As a manager, do you want to do a good management job, know your job well, be looked on as a good manager (relating), get a better post with a better car, or be respected as a good manager? Are all these motivating goals, and if so in what order of importance? The choice is yours. Clearly defined goals are so important to your eventual success that it is worth giving them a lot of thought, and the Life Content model is a useful tool.

NEUROLOGICAL LEVELS

Another model I have adapted successfully to goal-achieving relates to the thinking or neurological level at which change takes place, and to some extent reflects the hierarchy of goals we have already met. In this case, at a basic level, our goals concern the physical environment around us and our actual behaviour. At a much higher level, we are concerned with our identity, and with more spiritual values. This model was developed by Robert Dilts and has been applied to learning and change generally, as well as to problem-solving. Here I am applying it to the different levels at which our outcomes are ranked.

Environment

This concerns outside things we react to, our surroundings, and other people. You might want a better house or office, for instance, or to work nearer home, or to have a different boss.

Behaviour

This concerns what you do, rather than external factors. You might, for instance, want to make a particularly good job of a report or presentation for the managing director, or to negotiate an especially good deal with a client.

Capability

Capability concerns not just what you actually do, but what you are capable of, and the skills and strategies you use. You might want, for example, to be more computer literate, or to be able to read a balance sheet, or speak German, or to be more consistent in what you do.

Beliefs

On a day-to-day basis we have beliefs that either help or hinder us in what we do, or what we are capable of. They form our perceptions, for instance, of what is true, necessary, beneficial or harmful. These beliefs can either affect our goals indirectly, empowering or constraining us, or take the form of internal goals themselves – an inner conviction that you are ready for promotion, or would do well running an overseas subsidiary, for example, can be a strong, self-fulfilling belief, even if not consciously identified or adopted as such.

Identity

Your basic sense of self – your core values and mission in life – equates to the higher-level 'being' category in the Life Content model – 'I want to be a writer', 'I am a natural leader'.

The spiritual level

This is the deepest neurological level, at which the big questions such as Why are we here? What is our purpose? are addressed. This is where we have our sense of life purpose.

This model of neurological levels is another way you can put your goals into categories, and test them out. Typically, an outcome will have significance at more than one level. What seems to be a specific behavioural or environment issue, for instance, might really be to do with your capabilities. For example, maybe it's not where you are fishing that is wrong, or what happened once – or six times – but the fact that you haven't really got the skills you need. Or, at higher levels, you don't believe it's worth the time and effort (belief), or 'it's just not me' (identity), or 'what's the point of it all, anyway' (purpose or spiritual). Each higher neurological level controls lower levels. Thus, your behaviour may be affected by your capabilities, which in turn are affected by what you believe, which in turn will tend to fit how you see yourself, which will tend to fit any overriding purpose you have in life. Making changes to your behaviour, therefore, usually involves change at least one level higher.

Specific goals may have to be reconciled as between these levels, as was the case in the simple personal hierarchy, illustrated in Figure 3. If you don't 'see yourself' (identity) as a top manager, it is unlikely that your skills and eventual behaviour will match your longer-term outcome, so your short-term efforts will be wasted. You could have been doing things that

were more congruent with the values at your higher neurological levels, and by doing so would have had a far greater
chance of success. So-called high achievers have the uncanny
skill of matching what they do, and even the environment in
which they do it (including friends and colleagues), with their
identity and higher direction and values. This means there is
an economy of effort, a high hit rate of achieving what they set
out to do, and also the pleasure that comes from doing what
they really want to do. Understanding this model enables every
one of us to act with similar congruence and fulfilment.

These are different ways to consider the first stage in the four-
part success cycle – deciding what you want. Consistent goal-
achievers operate successful 'strategies', although these differ
from person to person, just as do the approaches we have
already met. Regardless of the content of your goals, you can
develop your own successful strategies – a process that will
work again and again.

One approach may make a lot more sense to you than
others. There may be value, however, in thinking from various
points of view. At worst, you will focus more on what you want,
and get more direction into your life. You may want to change
what you spend most of your time on, getting a better balance
between work, career, hobbies and interests, and important
relationships. Then you can concentrate on how best to
achieve the important goals you decide are most worthwhile.
In the next chapter we shall apply some specific tests to each
of these goals to increase *several times over* their chances of
fulfilment.

5

Testing for a Well-Formed Outcome

THERE are several simple tests you can apply to any goals which will dramatically increase your chances of success. These 'criteria for well-formed outcomes' have been applied successfully in all sorts of organisational contexts, but they have great impact at an individual level. You can start by applying them to any goals you have already identified in your own hierarchy. Once you have found them to be effective, you can apply equivalent tests to any work-based plans, group tasks, or business unit strategies.

You may have used a similar process before, perhaps in business planning – which is fine, as it is all common sense, and we can't have too much of that. As well as in a business or organisational sense, however, think about the criteria that follow also in personal terms, which is the main NLP application, and also in relation to the presuppositions we met earlier.

Is your goal specific?

Some goals are more like dreams or wishes, and have little chance of success. The more you can be specific, the greater the chance of realising your goal. A typical company mission statement, couched in general terms, and without reference to quantifiable criteria for success, would probably not pass the test of being specific. If the mission is supported by appropriate lower level goals and objectives, however, these will drive the business, rather than the mission statement, which will serve, perhaps, to rally staff and define corporate identity.

Know exactly what you want

The 'specific' test can be applied in many ways. You may have a personal goal to learn Spanish, for instance. This aspiration would not satisfy the 'specific' criterion, as there are many levels of language skill. Do you simply want to scrape through on your two-week holiday, or do you need a higher level? Does the standard have to enable you to live and work in a Spanish-speaking country, perhaps using the language to negotiate contracts? The choice is yours, but without specific goals your wishes are unlikely to materialise.

Decide on a timescale

Being specific usually means putting a timescale on your goal, rather than leaving it open-ended. In a corporate situation this test usually differentiates operational, quantifiable objectives from higher goals or a mission. Some outcomes, of the mission type, are nice to have and comprise pleasant words. Other outcomes incorporate measurable results, commitment and accountability. Resolving to produce material results by Friday at five o'clock concentrates the mind more than deciding to be 'a supplier of quality'. But as we saw, a congruent hierarchy of goals has to apply, to ensure that different 'parts' of you or your organisation are pulling in the same direction – whether to produce consistent quality, gain market share or achieve personal peace of mind. In terms of the four-part success cycle, the more clearly defined your target is, the more you will be able to tell how far you have missed it, and the more obvious will be the corrective action needed. In terms of the cybernetic model, the human system, acting mostly below the conscious level, seems to respond best to a clear, vivid goal.

Applying this test to the management goal 'Stop the decline in sales', you might define your desired outcome more clearly as 'Stop the decline in sales [volume, revenue?] of X product [or in Y region, depending on the specific goal] by the end of next quarter [or other reasonable timescale]'. In addition, you may decide that you want to change the product mix; and what about margins and discounts? Will you be satisfied just to stop the decline, or do you want to start an upward trend?

How will you know you have succeeded?

The more specific your goal, the more likely it is that you will be able to see, hear and feel the evidence that you have achieved it. Having tangible evidence of success is an important criterion, especially in terms of individual motivation, which is critical also to organisational success. It demands that your goal be specific in sensory terms as well as in words and resolutions. By expressing and *experiencing* your goal in sensory terms – seeing and feeling it as part of the planning process – it will act as a motivator in a way that a hazy wish or even a written-down goal will not. This internal experience then becomes the target that your cybernetic system will pursue until it becomes reality. And as well as providing internal motivation, you will also have evidence to show the world you have reached your outcome – this is an important factor for many people.

Sensory evidence

In many cases the evidence of having achieved your goal will be obvious. If you make your Spanish goal a pass at GCSE, you will get sensory evidence in the form of a visible, tangible certificate to prove what you have achieved. Other kinds of achievement have standard forms of evidence, such as a bank statement or sales report, but in other cases you may have to invent sensory evidence to make your outcome more robust, and this may require a little creativity. If your goal is to lose some weight – perhaps to reach eleven stone – you can rely on well-calibrated bathroom scales. A work-based task might include a written report or other document as an end product, or may involve performance measurements that can be expressed in numerical or money terms. Businesses have plenty of yardsticks for success, so applying this principle at work should not be difficult.

External yardsticks

At a personal level you may have to devise different ways of measuring, say health-related or family-related goals, in order to give them a tangible end result. If you like to jog, for instance, you can measure your progressive improvement in speed over the same course, and pulse rate will give extra evidence of how your body is improving. The goal of 'being a better parent' may need specific commitments to spend more time with your children, involving actual sensory evidence. Selling your house may require a sold sign outside. Financial goals may involve banked cheques, and a sporting goal may involve a handicap, actual scores or a position on the club ladder. You may have aspirations to write short stories, but by making your goal publication – even if only at a local level in some publication or other – your goal will take on a new vitality. If you are a painter maybe you should aim to exhibit or sell your work, as this will provide both tangible and external evidence of your success. If your objective is some reorganisation in the office, perhaps of the filing or other systems, decide on the end product and the hard evidence of success – which as it happens also provides useful ammunition when making a case for any change.

How will I know?

When you become familiar with the idea of requiring evidence, you will automatically build it into your goals. And it is better to do this *before* you embark on your goal, rather than part-way through. The more motivators you have to get you started, then keep you going, the better. Ask yourself: 'How exactly will I know I have fully achieved what I set out to achieve?' What will be the *sensory evidence* that might apply to this outcome, or as a spin-off benefit, and what would be the most attractive and motivating? However simplistic it may seem, this is one of the secrets of consistent achievement.

The sensory evidence for a business goal such as achieving a certain level of sales is easy, and the more specific the goal, the easier it will be to identify evidence. But as a manager you might want to have copy invoices, or even a debtor listing showing what has been collected, rather than a higher level report, a verbal presentation by the sales manager, or some on-line access via your personal computer.

Is your goal at the right level?

The size of your goal is critical. Too small, and you may not even be motivated sufficiently to get started. Too big and you may be scared to do anything, possibly busying yourself with activity related to the job but not getting you your outcome. This, of course, is a matter of perception, and one person will take in his stride a job which terrifies another.

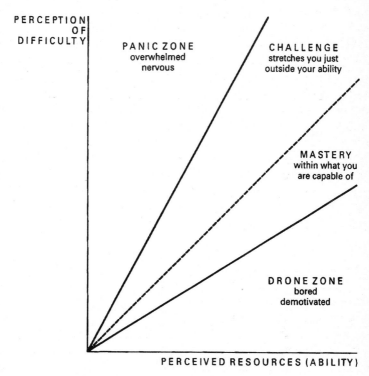

FIGURE 5 The peak performance zone

Optimum performance threshold

We each have an optimum threshold at which we work best. Many managers need to feel challenged or stretched before they give of their best. When working at our peak level we can be in a state of 'flow', in which productivity rises dramatically and nothing seems to stand in the way of success. This is when mastery happens, and where we learn very quickly. Usually a task or project can be broken down into convenient parts, or a longer project into time intervals, in such a way that each phase is both realistic and challenging. In a team situation it should not be difficult to do this, matching the tasks with the strengths and preferences of individuals. Figure 5 shows the relationship between these perceptions, and the different performance zones in which we operate.

The time dimension

Time is one dimension which can be used as a convenient variable for defining the optimum size of goal, just as in the case of making it specific. For instance, in the case of your Spanish qualification, you can fix the exam date to make the goal possible but also demanding, so that your motivation stays high. This will depend of course on other things you are doing over the same period. Even a minor extra goal can create stress when it competes with a lot of other commitments. So consider the effect on other goals in your hierarchy.

Chunking up or down

Sort out the level of your goals up front, so that you don't fail because of the size of the task, and so your success track record gets better and better. The process of goal achievement is one that can be learned. The learning process means that you will be able to make your goals bigger and more challenging each time. This is termed 'chunking up', or 'stepping up', in NLP. You can chunk a task up by making it bigger or more demanding, or perhaps having a tighter deadline. Or you can chunk it down, making it smaller in content or complexity, or with an easier deadline. The size of the task, both in terms of how you perceive the difficulty of the job, and how you perceive your own ability and resources, should be at the right level to motivate you personally. Remember that 'difficulty' is just a perception – most of us know what it is to feel out of our depth, when panic sets in. But when we break down the task into manageable chunks, or simply see it in the light of a new day, our perceptions can change. NLP is all about managing these thought processes, representing situations in an empowering way, and taking control of our behaviour and achievement.

The level of the sales goal, for example, may have to be got right. Do you want to stop the rate of decline, restore performance to where it was a year ago, or do you really want to turn the situation around and improve results? If so, by how much?

By ten per cent, or two hundred per cent? And is the end of the quarter realistic? Why not by the end of the year, or the end of the month? Will the target get your adrenaline flowing, or will it just create panic and depression? That is where size becomes important.

Is your goal positive?

We have already seen that it is better to express your goals in a positive rather than a negative way. Rather than 'lose half a stone', why not set your goal as being to reach a specified weight by a certain date? It does not cost you anything to reframe your outcome, and the brain does not have to cope with the nasty idea of losing anything. Do this from the moment your goals are conceived, and certainly when you come to write them down. This principle can apply in any work context, at any level. For example, rather than simply trying to avoid excess inventory or other working capital, decide what levels you actually want and state them positively, perhaps as ratios. This simple skill will become a habit, and in time your whole attitude will become more positive – something that, for many managers, generations of training and development training has failed to achieve.

Hits rather than misses

This is more than just a matter of semantics. The human brain seems to work better with positives than with negatives. Although our goal-achieving mechanisms are staggeringly sophisticated, the message to the brain can sometimes be misunderstood if expressed in a negative form. Any parent who has admonished their child 'don't spill that', or 'don't miss', will know how only the negative, operative words 'spill' and 'miss' seem to register, so the opposite result to that intended is achieved. The same strange principle is at work when you learn to ride a bike, when it seems all the 'don'ts' are a waste of breath, as far as the brain is concerned. So decide what you want to hit rather than what you want to miss. You may want to avoid bankruptcy, or take-over, or falling sales, or low morale. Fine, but what would you like instead? What is the target you want to *hit*, rather than the infinite number of non-targets you want to miss?

Tricking the brain

Try not to think about your nostrils. Be honest: to *not* think about them you had to first think about them. For practical purposes the brain can only cope with positive ideas. It is humanly impossible not to imagine your boss in a bright yellow, undersized jumper without first internally representing (seeing, in this case) the positive image. And the harder you try not to imagine the image, the more you will imprint it. So rather than set a goal not to have your house repossessed, make it positive: to pay off the mortgage or the arrears, or a smaller positive step in the right direction. Business goals need not sound like fire-fighting, skin-of-the-teeth survival measures. Switch into a positive mode to trick your brain into positive, empowering associations.

Pleasure rather than pain

Underlying every behaviour is the basic desire for pleasure, and to avoid pain. The positive principle means we should set out to gain pleasure, rather than avoid pain. Somehow, although the net effect might seem to be the same, thinking in positive terms works better when achieving goals. If you have difficulty expressing a goal positively, ask yourself 'What would I rather have?' There may be some other positive outcome which is more attractive than the negative outcome you have set.

The sales outcome illustration to stop the decline in sales is of course the wrong way round. A positive goal will be to achieve a certain level of sales by a certain date. Even if the outcome means just lowering a downward trend, or has only a marginal effect, it can still be expressed in positive terms.

What will you do to achieve your goal?

Goals that are outside your control or influence are unlikely to happen, at least in any consistent or predictable way. NLP is not about mind over matter, but involves practical realities. Well-formed outcomes depend upon you doing something yourself – something more than just dreaming and visualising – to ensure success. However altruistic you may be in setting goals on behalf of others, such as your family or your company, you may be on a hiding to nothing if you have little or no part in their fulfilment. You may want your child to do well in school, college or in their career, for example, but with the best will in the world your goal may not happen. It depends on somebody else. However, you can perhaps revise your goal in such a way that your action makes it happen. For example, you may be able to give your child specific help, such as in the education you provide, personal help, or a financial start in business. Your goal concerns the part that *you* play, and you should measure your success against that.

Getting results through people

This principle is particularly important in an organisation, and in the case of managers who get results through other people. The important factors are influence and authority. If you have control over resources and the power to get people to do what you want, then it is within your power to achieve big goals that involve other people – perhaps many. But a junior manager would be unlikely to pull off a corporate-level goal, and a first-line manager may not have the power to undertake a task that his senior manager boss could.

Influencing a team

In a sports context, it would be unrealistic for the goalkeeper or striker to set himself the goal of getting the team into the first division. Even a brilliant season on his part might not bring about promotion. But such a goal could well be realistic for the captain or manager of the team, with the authority and influence to make it happen. So ask yourself 'What can I do to bring about my goal?' The goalkeeper need not be disappointed. He can set himself a positive target of increasing his record of saves, and the striker can set himself a straightforward goals-scored target. Each in turn does their own part, and together the team will do wonders. As a manager your part might be to influence, persuade or coach – in fact, to manage. Playing this role to the full, you will be able to bring about major goals within your organisation. Just make sure you are the key player in achieving your goals, whatever the talents and apparent commitment of others, and that no person or group has the power to wreck your goals.

Because of their massive reliance on other people, this principle is particularly crucial for top managers. Outcomes of corporate significance aren't usually achieved by one-man bands, whereas lower down the company hierarchy, managers can shine through achieving specific tasks or projects individually. For this reason, communication skills become increasingly critical in the higher levels of leadership. But given the influence and authority that comes with position, these skills – any skills – can be acquired, and in this sense are within the control of the individual. Any of these factors may affect this outcome test, so you will need a good dose of common sense and judgement.

In the case of the sales example, stop the decline in sales, such an outcome would probably have to be brought about by the sales manager, if overall performance was improve. And even in this case, he or she would have to identify things to do personally – if only in the form of incentives or motivation – to bring about the result. An individual sales representative could, however, have a well-formed outcome in respect of his own territory.

Have you got the resources?

Given that you are responsible for your own success, have you got what it takes? In a corporate context, resources can be a crucial element in goal achievement. Without the necessary financial investment, for instance, certain ambitious goals will be out of the question – and this will apply with respect to plant, people or skills. These can all be acquired, however, perhaps over a period, so can represent interim outcomes. In other words, a lack of *acquirable* resources, including skills and knowledge, need not be a critical factor in your success. If you need £1000 to do what you have to do, first set yourself the goal of getting that sum of money. If you don't have the time to do this, make it your goal to make the time. If the management controls you need require a special computer system, make it your first goal to design or choose the system and get it set up. All this is consistent with a hierarchy of goals – little goals contributing to big ones; short-term goals helping towards longer-term goals; and all going in the direction of your organisation's mission.

Innate and acquirable resources

The same applies to some extent at a personal level. You may not have the skill to undertake a big goal, but you can acquire it. You can learn what has to be learned. You can bridge the gap from your present state to the state you want to be, one step at a time. So at this personal level the test applies more to *innate* resources rather than those that can be acquired. A goal you might set yourself at the age of fifty might, sadly, be unrealistic, whatever money you can get or whatever skills you can acquire at that age. But a younger person might happily pass this test. Similarly there are things a six-footer can achieve that a five-foot stripling would be unwise to contemplate. Fortunately, surprisingly few goals are out of reach simply by virtue of lack of innate resources – all the time extraordinary feats are achieved against all the odds. But be prepared to apply the test, if need be using a trusted friend to let you know if you have not got what it takes.

A salesperson will usually have the innate resources to achieve higher performance. Often top sales performers are far from representing the salesperson stereotype, and achieve their success through sheer determination, single-mindedness, or ambition. With a positive state of mind, skill resources can be quickly acquired. Physical resource deficits that might hamper the goal (like running out of stock, or the van breaking down) can be addressed as outcomes in their own right (get inventory level/production up, get van repaired). The rule of thumb in this case is always to assume that you have the resources, or can get them, until you are fully convinced otherwise: 'If anyone can, I can.' We usually underestimate our potential.

Ecology: what or who else might be affected?

We have considered ecology, the framework surrounding the change-of-state model. Few goals happen in isolation. One may be a prerequisite of another, or may be affected in some way by another. The success of any organisational plans, for example, will depend upon how they are broken down into parts and coordinated. Otherwise, functions and departments will be pulling in different directions, and resources will be wasted. No goal is an island.

Vertical and horizontal congruence

The need for coordination applies on two dimensions in an organisation of any size. First, it applies vertically, as low-level plans are integrated with higher-level ones to produce a single company master plan, hopefully in line with a broad mission statement. Part of this process is the reconciling of parochial, functional or departmental demands and intentions with the big picture – not least, the resources needed to achieve the plan.

Secondly there also needs to be congruence horizontally, as between parts, regions or functions of the company. Typically all sorts of historical and cultural hurdles will have to be overcome in this process, and as much company politics as economic or marketing rationale is likely to be involved. The framework of interdependence of all the outcomes is the 'ecology' we met earlier in the change-of-state model. This is analogous with the natural ecology, in which any change has an effect on the wider environment. So in NLP terms this is an 'ecology test', and it has wide importance.

Personal vs. work goals

Ecology is an even bigger factor at a personal level. First of all other goals might be affected by any given outcome. For instance, a decision to work long hours or perhaps over the weekend for company or even career reasons might conflict with a family or social goal. A goal to do with studying for qualifications might clash with one to complete a work project, or take part in sport. Secondly, our goals might conflict with those of other people that we care about – again, whether in a work, social or domestic context. The ecology principle works as between our own various goals and those of other people, just as it does between the many goals in your own life.

Following on from this, it is not in our long-term interest to 'use' others unfairly to bring about our chosen outcomes. Ultimately, such a policy does not work, just as misuse of the natural environment exacts its own eventual cost.

Positive intentions

At a personal level the ecology criterion may have a further significance. We have already met the presupposition that behind every behaviour there is a positive intention. As we saw, some of these intentions – or outcomes – may operate unconsciously. It is possible therefore that these will conflict with conscious goals, so that both are affected. A conscious decision to stop working at weekends might be competing with an unarticulated desire to please the boss, be 'one of the girls', ward off possible failure as work piles up, and so on. Conversely, a rational outcome of gaining a part-time degree might conflict with unconscious intentions concerned with the many other things you could be doing with your time – immediate work demands, caring for an aged relative, or nurturing a faltering marriage.

By their nature, unconscious 'drivers' do not get the rational attention of our conscious goals, but in practice they often become the dominant force, thus wrecking otherwise well-planned goals. NLP techniques help us to identify these intentions, which in some respects reflect the many sides of our personality, and certainly the two sides of our brain – logical and intuitive.

Who or what else will they affect?

A little thought, however, will usually identify outcomes which might conflict with those you have written down. Ask yourself, for instance, 'What would happen if I got this?' Or, 'If I could get it straight away, would I take it?' Or 'Who else would this affect?' A goal to become managing director, for instance, might cause you some trepidation if you were offered the contract and keys to start on Monday. The causes of your trepidation will reflect other intentions that are in conflict. You may not be ready to make public speeches, to take issue with the chairman, to come to terms with balance sheets and to find your way around the City. You might be unwilling to risk failure. Or you might not be ready to give up the familiarity and relationships in your present role. These are harsh but common-sense tests about your true outcomes.

The bottom line is that we can't have it all ways. Outcomes not only have to be specific and realistic, but you have to be going in one direction, your outcomes supporting rather than competing with each other. If your answer to the MD offer, or any other goal, is 'Yes, but. . .' you may have to get the ecology of your goals sorted out. Get them into priority ranking, in the form of a hierarchy, so that you can see where you are going overall and can easily spot those goals that are stopping you achieving more important ones.

In the declining sales example other goals may be at work. For example, the margins on additional sales may not be worth the bother and you would be better without the offending product, or market. Tackling the issue of sales only may be delaying the agony, and you may have to shut up shop in any event. The sales manager may have to work even longer hours and his marriage is already at breaking point. Or he might want to get rid of a representative and needs another couple of months' poor performance as ammunition. Or he is planning a management buyout, and the last thing he wants is to boost the sales. An ecology check puts your outcomes in a holistic frame, and protects your *overall* outcome.

WHAT TO DO

All of this can be translated into action. If you have not already done so, try putting your goals into order in the form of a hierarchy. Start by just listing everything you want to get, do, be, or know, using the Life Contents model, and applying the tests. At this stage, any goals and wishes can be included. As you think about longer-term aims, be ready to include higher or longer-term goals and purposes to do with self-fulfilment, your special identity, and basic contentment. Then try to fit them all into a cascade diagram, or hierarchy, with higher-level, long-term goals at the top, and the goals supporting them at each level below. A second-tier goal of financial independence might have several subordinate goals below it, such as 'get final qualification', get deputy post, save so much each month. Each of these will in turn have their own supporting goals and specific tasks, right down to 'send off for forms', 'get report in on Thursday', 'agree agenda with Liz', and so on. All your outcomes on daily or weekly 'to do' lists will integrate with higher-level goals. If they don't, ask yourself why you are putting in the time and effort in the first place. If the lower levels of your hierarchy do not identify *actual* things to do *straight away*, maybe you need to go back over the tests and make your goals more specific and within your immediate control.

Reconciling work and non-work goals

As long as you are working for a company, you will have to adopt some or all of the organisation's goals as your own. If you cannot, maybe on ethical grounds, the hierarchy exercise is already doing its job as you have an early warning to get your personal values and priorities sorted out. You may be on a hiding to nothing pursuing different goals – sooner or later something will give and you may not succeed either at work or away from it.

Alternatively, you may be able to adjust your goals so that they are coherent and make 'ecological' sense. Whatever the conflicts at the lower levels (say, whether you should work late or attend your child's school sports day), at a higher level your goals will merge. To 'be happy' will mean achieving outcomes in every area of your life, as we are unable to plan our lives in watertight compartments, at least in terms of states of mind.

Applying the 'well-formed outcome' criteria

Having constructed your personal hierarchy of goals, the next job, which you may have started as you were reading through, is to apply the above tests to each of your outcomes. The wishes and pipedreams may then be eliminated because they are neither specific, nor within your control, or you just cannot see yourself fulfilling them. Others you thought you were committed to might also fail one or more tests, and you are left with the decision of whether to go ahead given a low proba-bility of achievement. Some goals might evolve and become clearer, and others will be easily amended to meet the important criteria. Some which are fine in their own right fail the ecology test, and will either have to be amended – perhaps changing the timescale until an interim goal has been carried out – or abandoned. What you will be left with is individual goals that have a good chance of achievement, and a hierarchy of goals that is coherent and ecologically sound.

Paradoxically, using the 'well-formed criteria' will probably remove some of the long term but vital goals to do with identity and self-fulfilment. The goal 'to be happy', for instance, might fail several tests – it is certainly not specific. The outcomes that will bring about your ultimate desired state are those that are specific enough to actually change your behaviour. They will usually include some evidence that can be seen, felt or heard. The process is a self-correcting one, if you always keep within the hierarchy and ecology frame. If you've got it right, your higher aims will be the natural consequence of achieving more specific, measurable or at least observable goals. The process is also self-fulfilling, as what we think about most tends to be what actually happens – subjective thought becomes objective reality. So this is not a theoretical planning exercise. Real behaviours, and tangible outcomes, come about through this process of goal-identification. Be honest and rigorous in applying the tests. Well-formed outcomes have an uncanny habit of becoming reality, so the potential winnings are enormous if you get this part right. Being specific and personally responsible means of course that you can't easily avoid blame if things go wrong. But if you are not ready to risk the odd failure and the responsibility that goes with it, there is little chance of success anyway. Keep the presuppositions in mind. 'We all work perfectly'; 'If anyone can, I can'.

6

Creative Visualisation

MOST of what we have considered so far has been a logical and partly analytical look at outcomes. The human mind uses two very different kinds of operating system when cybernetically achieving the goals we set it. We use the logical left brain to do the sort of tests we have just covered, using language or symbolism, such as numbers – which is a left-brain specialisation – to express things and 'think' them through. The right brain, on the other hand, deals in non-linguistic representation associated with creative imagination, intuition and visualisation. When we talk about having vision, having a dream, or a brainwave, it is probably the creative right brain at work.

In terms of specific goals, to form a clear picture of what you are going to do or get – to imagine what something will be like – draws on right-brain powers. In practice, of course, we use both sides of the brain all the time – it is just that each side does its own special jobs better than the other, so is largely left to get on with it, just as your right and left hands do in everyday tasks. And as with 'handedness', one side may be dominant. It seems, for instance, that most managers are more at home with left-brain logical, sequential thinking than with their creative and somewhat mystical right brain.

Self-fulfilling mental imagery

The significance of this in terms of outcomes is that we have to harness the whole mind to bring about what we want. So if we are left-brain dominant, right-brain creativity will need to be stimulated. The 'target' in the cybernetic goal-achieving system to which I have already referred is reinforced by right-brain imagery. In effect we *create* a goal in imagery – as an electro-chemical neural network, forming a 'target blueprint' – before it can become objective reality. Hence the clear picture, or better still, a full synaesthetic representation of what you want to achieve, complete with sights, sounds, feelings, tastes and smells.

Habitual worriers have perfected this technique of inner visualisation, and are able to effectively 'live out' the most improbable scenarios, thus creating their future. It should be no surprise, when we understand the way we respond cybernetically to this mental imagery, that to a large extent our thoughts are self-fulfilling. A positive person produces positive outcomes; a negative person produces negative outcomes. 'An accident waiting to happen' is an everyday illustration of how this manifests itself. And 'Whatsoever a man thinketh, so he is', confirms the timeless wisdom of this human phenomenon. One feature of top leaders and successful sportspeople is the way they 'live out' successes mentally long before they become reality, acting out a sort of blueprint or mental rehearsal. Although it is a natural human characteristic, this is a learned thinking skill and is an important part of some NLP techniques.

In terms of electro-chemical happenings in the brain, or at the synaptic level, there does not seem to be much difference between a clearly imagined outcome and the real thing. This is apparent, of course, not just in the inveterate worriers I have referred to, but in the case of vivid dreams, which can be as real as any kind of reality. But the brain can be equally absorbed whenever we are taken up with our own inner thought world, in what is termed 'downtime'.

So not only does right-brain imagery make our goals more robust, as many top sportspeople will testify, but it is part of the very system that enables us to achieve them. Without it, we are no more likely to achieve what we want than a missile is to do its job without the target first being programmed into it. 'I can't imagine that happening' is not just a self-fulfilling prophecy, as the positive thinkers would tell us, but it confirms that the inner goal has not even been programmed.

Right-brain imagery in goal achievement

This has special significance for goal-achievement, with a number of implications:

- Goals are not just useful – they are crucial; in the human cybernetic system all behaviour depends on them.
- There are far more powerful ways to 'register' our goals than just writing them down.
- Outcomes can be created internally in any degree of detail you wish, and in effect you can experience them before they happen. So-called scenario planning requires this sort of skill. You can test out different outcomes before committing resources or taking risks.
- We can internally experience states of mind, as well as people, things and places. So the 'change of state' model makes a lot of sense.
- Visualisation as a technique can be used to make an outcome more compelling – that is, as a motivator. This involves 'tuning' the various submodalities, or character- istics of our imagined outcome, such as the brightness or focus of the picture or the loudness of the sound. (See Figure 6 on page 68.) In this way you can literally motivate yourself.
- Internalising your goal in this way enables subconscious associations to do with your outcome to be brought into play. It triggers the target-seeking system.
- This is consistent with the well-known idea of unconscious competence, in which skills operate without effort on your part, but nonetheless according to some internalised goal.
- There can be *degrees* of clarity. A goal can be compelling, having vivid and realistic sensory representations, or less attractive and typically having less clearly focused imagery. These degrees can be changed to prioritise otherwise random outcomes. *Conscious* priorities are thus translated into behaviour, rather than habitual behaviour (which may follow unconscious intentions) becoming the master.
- There is no need to visualise *how* you will achieve the goal. In fact, prescribing in detail how you will get there will limit your flexibility in following intuitive, subconscious associations.
- A clearly visualised goal is more readily communicated to other people.

VISUAL

Brightness	Contrast
Size	Clarity
Colour/black & white	Focus
Saturation (vividness)	Framed/panoramic
Hue or colour blance	Movement
Shape	Perspective
Locations	Associated/dissociated
Distance	3-dimensional/flat

AUDITORY

Pitch	Duration
Tempo (speed)	Location
Volume	Distance
Rhythm	External/internal
Continuous/interrupted	Source
Timbre or tonality	Mono/stereo
Digital (words)	Clarity
Associated/dissociated	Number

KINAESTHETIC (Sensations)

Pressure	Movement
Location	Duration
Number	Intensity
Texture	Shape
Temperature	Frequency (tempo)

FIGURE 6 Modalities and submodalities

Mental rehearsal

Outcomes can be tested in a logical way, using the criteria in Chapter 5, and they can also be set and strengthened as internal sensory representations. This process of representing or imagining a future is termed 'future pacing' in NLP, and more widely, mental rehearsal. As an NLP technique it has various applications in addition to goal-setting, some of which you will meet later.

The practice of mental rehearsal predates NLP and, for example, remarkable results have been achieved by sportspeople who use mental imagery to prepare for an event. In some research, improvements in performance differed little between those who practised normally and those who 'practised' internally. Similarly salespeople have increased their output using these techniques, sometimes described as mental role-playing. Any sportsperson must come to terms with putting earlier misses, or failures out of their mind when facing the next race, tee or challenge. And the same problem applies to giving a speech or conducting a training session.

The unique feature of mental rehearsal as a conscious goal-achieving technique is that you don't have to register 'misses' or failures of any kind. In this way the brain can be made to experience the positive 'weighting' of successes, which accounts for the apparent confidence and lack of effort which those with a better mental attitude seem to display. Right-brain imagery counterbalances the critical, self-analytical left brain, and the whole brain does a far better job. The same phenomenon of left brain/right brain partnership, as it happens, can be found in human excellence of all kinds, including leadership and business.

Strategies for goal achievement

How we visualise goals plays a big part in what eventually we achieve. There is a difference between the way we structure 'goal thoughts' that we never seem to achieve, and those we succeed in. Successful patterns or structures of thought can be used again and again to bring about repeated success, whatever the nature and content of the goals themselves. So, for example, you often find you can adapt successful strategies from a hobby or sport for use in your work life, and vice versa. Even if you excel in a single field only, this can be used as a basis to improve your performance in other areas in which your self-image and confidence are low. Having done this, you are then free to elicit the successful strategies of others as well. Part Four covers these successful strategies in more detail. For the moment, it is important to practise visualisation to reinforce your well-formed outcomes.

_____ **EXERCISE** _____

Making your goals reality

Choose one or two goals high up on your priority list and visualise them as completed outcomes. The earlier tests will have been good preparation, as unless your goals are specific, or you can imagine sensory evidence of your goals, it will not be easy to make your images clear. Similarly, unless you are the main player, you will not feature much in the mental screenplay you create and direct. It may be helpful to go through each modality separately, first of all seeing the sights, then hearing all the sounds, then experiencing the feelings. Then bring them together to form a total, realistic experience, which is what gives the goal-achieving power.

You may well find that one or more of your goals is easy to visualise, and the imagery is clear and in focus, whereas others are more difficult to imagine. You can use the specific mental qualities or submodalities of what is a real burning desire – a goal you are confident of achieving, and which you find motivating and pleasurable – as a model for others you want to achieve but which are little more than wishes or pipedreams, and which are neither 'well-formed' nor compelling. Simply switch the submodalities – that is, the detailed characteristics of the sights, sounds and feelings – whatever form they take, from the compelling image to the less clear one. You can use Figure 6 as a checklist. Practise identifying and changing these characteristics – this will give you an enormous edge in taking control over the state you are in and achieving the outcomes you set.

◄ PART THREE ►

Understanding Communication

7

Communicating for Results

'THE meaning of a communication is the response it produces' – we met this presupposition in Chapter 3. As with any behaviour, communication has its purpose; we do it for a reason – to inform, persuade, scare or whatever. So everything we have learned about outcomes, and how to make them clearer or more robust, applies equally to communication. One important outcome for any communication, regardless of its specific purpose and content, is rapport, which is a key factor in successful communication. NLP shows how vital rapport can be established and maintained.

This part of the book looks at some of the ways in which we differ, in thought and behaviour, and at the many filters that make our mental maps mutually hard to understand. I then describe ways in which we can identify and allow for these differences, in order to build and maintain rapport. Effective communication follows from this, and, more importantly, the outcomes we desire. I also examine, in Chapter 11, a major language model known as the Meta Model, which helps to derive more precise meaning from everyday communication.

NLP offers a number of techniques that can help improve our communication, but the secret does not lie principally in techniques. A clear outcome, and an understanding of the four-stage process of achieving outcomes – any outcome, including a communication one – will be of more value than a whole portfolio of techniques and systems. And nor can we rely on the sophistication of our technology and equipment. Techniques and high-tech methods, however, may well enhance a communication that is based on the common-sense principles we have looked at.

As a manager, you may be accustomed to using various kinds of communication, with little reference to their appropriateness to specific outcomes. In each case there may be room for improvement in skill. And in each case you might well ask whether a more appropriate medium or type of communication would do the job better, or indeed whether the 'communication' is needed at all to achieve your outcome. The following are examples:

- telephone calls
- group presentations
- one-to-one personal meetings
- casual face-to-face communication
- formal speeches
- contributing as part of a discussion group
- contributing in a more formal meeting
- training a group
- coaching an individual
- fax transmissions
- word-processed or typed memos
- e-mail transmissions
- hand-written notes
- chairing a meeting
- staff announcements
- formal warning letters
- disciplinary face-to-face meetings – both formal and informal
- written reports
- presentations of reports
- 'making a case', verbally or in writing
- visiting a client or supplier.

There is a lot of choice in this selection. It is not always obvious which is the best kind of communication to achieve your ultimate outcome under given circumstances, even though there are obvious cost, convenience and effectiveness pros and cons. Provided, however, that your outcome is clear and you keep it in mind, you should make the right choices, even if, in the case of recurring communications, some trial and error over a period is involved

Typically we *automatically* use the telephone for certain types

of communication, letters for others, and face-to-face meetings
for others – 'That's the way it's done, at least in our organisation.' Usually we do not give much thought to which is the
best way of achieving our *outcome* – if we have decided on an
outcome at all. Nor, in the case of most communications, do we
rigorously identify those that are not needed in the first place.
So, as we have already seen, it helps to identify your outcomes
in a hierarchical way, so that specific goals requiring some form
of communication will support a higher-level outcome.

Decide on your outcome

At one level the purpose of your communication might be to:

- persuade
- inform
- motivate to action (or inaction)
- consult
- impress
- warn
- delegate
- gain information
- understand feelings
- intimidate
- solicit opinions
- entertain
- propose
- encourage
- explain
- pacify
- counsel
- suggest
- frighten
- summarise.

At a more immediate level you might want to:

- persuade John to start the accounts sooner
- explain how the new appraisal scheme will affect the
  northern region
- suggest a better way of wording a report
- get little Amanda to sit still

And so on.

At a higher level you might want to:

- improve the sales results
- get a better job
- curry favour with the MD
- have an easy life
- reorganise the department.

And so on.

Matching outcome and medium

In each case, clearly identifying your outcome will give significance to the type of communication you choose. If you have something sensitive to get across to a member of your staff you might choose:

- a casual or apparently unplanned face-to-face meeting
- a planned meeting, formal or informal, on your patch or his, in work time or in a social setting
- a memo or hand-written note, informally or formally worded
- a light-hearted, humorous approach
- a more serious approach
- to communicate through another intermediate member of staff
- a shake of the head, raising of the eyebrows, grunt, or wave of the hand.

And so on.

In terms of achieving an outcome, the communication permutations that are available to you, notwithstanding all the organisational and financial constraints that managers usually bemoan, are limitless. And 'choice is better than no choice' when it comes to achieving outcomes. Such choice stems *naturally* from an outcome-based approach, not just to your communication but to tasks and goals generally. There is usually more than one route to get to your destination.

In practice, however, there may be more than one *destination*, or purpose to your communication. As well as passing on information you may also want to impress, persuade, or spur to action at the same time. But you may not pursue these other intentions *consciously*. So it may be helpful to consider the ecology of your main outcome, as I described in Chapter 5, as one of the tests of a good outcome. You may want to get across a strong disciplinary message to a member of the staff, maintain a valued social relationship, comply with company rules, while also communicating leadership qualities. So your choice of message, medium, location and style may have to be a compromise. But by focusing on what you want to achieve, and reconciling possible outcome conflicts, rather than on the mechanics of the communication, you are more likely to succeed.

Focus on what you want

Develop the routine practice of applying an outcome, or several, and some structure to every communication as an up-front investment. Ask yourself:

- What do I want to achieve?
- Are there any conflicting outcomes?
- What is the best way to get my message across?
- How can I achieve and maintain rapport?
- Am I the best person to communicate?
- How will they take it?

This routine can apply to the most innocuous casual communications, as well as to a major speech or written presentation. It makes no more sense to make a brief telephone call that is not really needed than to write a clever report that will not be understood or even read, and yet you are likely to make scores of such telephone calls habitually. 'Planning' might mean making no more than three or four scribbled points before a telephone call, mentally rehearsing what you want to achieve from your boss as you walk down the corridor, or spending the best part of a weekend drafting a speech which is important to your career. In each case the effort taken can be a wise investment. So decide *your* outcome, but choose the best medium and message to suit *the other person*.

The 'like' principle

One of the principles in establishing rapport is to be *like* the other person. This involves like *thinking*, and using the earlier analogy requires you to be willing to understand and share the others person's map of the world. The result is usually a win-win outcome. If, as a result of a similar upbringing and education, you have interests similar to the person you are communicating with – perhaps regarding sport, politics, or religion – there will be a common basis upon which to communicate. Alternatively, if the person's 'map' is very different as a result of being raised in a different culture and educational system, it may be less easy to establish rapport. But the 'like' principle in communication can apply in many other ways:

- an optimistic person will tend to hit it off with another optimist rather than a pessimist;
- a person who is punctilious in attending to detail may have difficulty relating to an easy-going person who tends to take a broad-brush approach;
- habitual worriers tend to get along fine together;
- a strongly visual person might not relate to a 'feelings' person;
- fast talkers – or slow talkers – relate well to others of similar style;
- action people don't usually hit it off with dreamers.

These are generalisations, but the 'like principle' is remarkably robust. Any exceptions tend to illustrate how skilled communicators can overcome basic mismatches *despite* differences. The onus is on the communicator to *create* the likeness and thus the necessary rapport.

Less obviously, we relate also in terms of physiological likeness. In effect, we like people to resemble us in appearance and behaviour, besides in their attitudes, beliefs and temperament. None of this necessarily takes place at a conscious level, but these factors are nonetheless an important part of the rapport process, and one we can learn about and use to our benefit. Excellent communication fits the same four-part success model we met in Chapter 2. It is about knowing what you want to achieve, and being flexible enough to change what you do. As we have seen, there are lots of ways to communicate, so you usually have choices. And you may need to use them: communicating means bridging mental maps, not just delivering a message from on high with the latest high-tech gadgetry. Achieving good communication is an awesome task, but is well repaid. The key is 'likeness' and rapport; in the next chapter we shall look at specific techniques to ensure this rapport.

8

The Magic of Rapport

IN this chapter I describe some specific principles and techniques that will help you gain that vital ingredient of good communication, rapport – the perception of likeness that can get you just about anything you want. Every communication will have an outcome, which will be unique to the circumstances and people involved. Your outcome is subject to the same goal-achieving principles we met in Chapter 4 and the common-sense tests in Chapter 5. But, whatever the circumstances or content of your communication outcome, establishing rapport should be high on your agenda.

MATCHING

One sign of rapport between people in conversation is that they tend to adopt the same physical posture and mannerisms – their silhouettes seem to suggest the same profile, as they talk at a street corner or lean over a desk towards each other. This is sometimes known as mirroring. Although we are rarely conscious of it in everyday communication, the phenomenon has been well researched and video recordings illustrate it starkly.

This matching may extend to a matching of speed, volume and tone of voice. Communicating with another person whose body language is very different from your own – perhaps sitting with crossed legs and arms in response to your open, positive posture – can be surprisingly difficult. Or imagine a conversation between a very fast talking person and a slow, reflective talker. All the nuances of facial expression, as well as the rest of your body posture and mannerisms, are included in this physiological matching. Our faces can present an open book, providing some of the feedback upon which interpersonal communication depends. Not only this, but facial matching – raising the eyebrows, or the other 101 facial expressions we use in everyday conversation – can create excellent rapport. When we *are* in rapport, all this comes naturally, of course, and we certainly do not think about what we are doing with our intricate facial muscles. However, applying the matching technique consciously (at first), we can establish or improve rapport that we would otherwise not have enjoyed.

Matching physiology, voice and other characteristics, then, is known to increase rapport and improve communication. But this works both ways. *Mismatching* physiology and voice characteristics are suggestive of poor rapport, and also act to reduce or curtail it. So mismatching is an effective way to bring a meeting or interview to a rapid close.

The best communicators match without thinking, certainly in any conscious sense, and you can observe it universally when people get on well together. The better the rapport – such as when people are in love – the closer the mirroring (a term sometimes used interchangeably with matching) of behaviour. This is a highly effective communication technique, but the skill needs to be developed to the extent that it becomes unconscious, or at least uncontrived.

Calibrating rapport

The principle can be used in different ways. As well as actively mirroring to increase rapport, by observing the other person for evidence of matching, you can determine the extent to which you have rapport – whether you are 'connecting', and whether they are paying attention. In NLP this is one aspect of what is termed *calibration*, and this is an example of the sensory acuity that I have already referred to. At the simplest level we can deduce from a smile or a frown what the other person is feeling. But there are countless less obvious non-verbal cues. So the degree of 'mirroring' can be a *measure* of rapport and effective communication. It is a by-product of having high rapport as well as a technique for improving rapport.

Matching in group situations

Matching also works in group situations. One person crosses their legs, and within not many minutes the rest are doing the same thing. One person leans forward with hands out on the table, and others soon follow. Often the boss or most influential person starts it off, so you can recognise where the power lies. Again this is more evident where there is rapport, and an individual who is 'anti' or who is preoccupied with their own thoughts will do their own physiological thing.

Crossover matching

The idea is so simple that many managers fail to appreciate the power of the process. To experience its effectiveness you need to first start watching others, and then try it out yourself. If the prospect of consciously mirroring is embarrassing or daunting, you can use a watered-down version sometimes known as crossover matching or mirroring. Just go part way. If someone folds their arms, cross your legs, for example. If they cup their chin in their hands, just touch your face with one hand. If they tap their pen, twirl yours. If they lean right forward, you can take a more open or neutral posture, and so on. This might be more comfortable for you, although it is most unlikely that the other person will be aware of what is happening, even in the case of very tight mirroring. So don't worry about the person, or others, noticing. This rarely happens. On the contrary, we become conscious and feel uneasy when others are *not* acting as we are, which usually means that rapport is broken, and communication is not working.

Voice and word matching

Matching need not be confined to facial expression and body posture; and I have already referred, for instance, to matching voice patterns. This includes speed or pace, pitch (high or low), and timbre (the amount of resonance). Word inflections also vary, and some people use and emphasise certain words repeatedly. These characteristics are part of their familiar way of representing things, and you can work wonders in rapport by using and emphasising the words and expressions they use.

Voice mirroring is important when it comes to telephone conversations, as you do not have the advantage of seeing all the body cues. The same effect in creating rapport, however, is possible with voice variables. People who are 'natural' on the telephone, and expert telesales people, do this with unconscious competence.

PACING AND LEADING

We tend to *follow* a person's physiology when it is changed. If a person in conversation crosses their arms, there is a good chance that the other person will do the same shortly afterwards. If a person leans back and clasps their hands behind their head, again it is extraordinary to watch the other person, quite unconsciously, take on a similar pose. This of course suggests that there is rapport between them and the communication is going well.

Using this principle, matching can be taken further and used in a more positive way. Once you have *paced* yourself to the person, you can then subtly *lead* them into a certain voice mode, facial expression or physiological posture with a view to changing their state of mind, whilst maintaining rapport. Often folding the arms and crossing the legs reflects a non-receptive frame of mind (but not always – it may just be a comfortable position). So, for example, by leading a person to a more open posture, you can actually induce a more positive, receptive mental state.

Incremental leading

Changes of physiology should be carried out incrementally, and not in an obvious way. The arms might first be unfolded, then, after the other person has followed suit, the legs uncrossed. This can be applied to speed and tone of voice, and to any other characteristics of the communication, including body position. In the case of a person who is irate, for example, and speaking quickly in a high-pitched voice, initially you will need to match their characteristics, at least to some degree – if you were to speak in a slow, controlled way that did not seem to reflect their feelings, you would be more likely to antagonise them. You start by being like them.

Having established reasonable rapport by pacing (and this will be achieved as much by mirroring body language as by any words you use) you can then gradually lead them in the way you want to. In the case of an angry person, you might incrementally slow down the speed of your speech, then perhaps slow down your arm gesticulations until you gradually lead them to do the same, maintaining rapport throughout. Not surprisingly, when people *act* in a less animated way their feelings will tend to match their behaviour – our state of mind and physiology are inextricably linked (are you happy because you whistle, or do you whistle because you're happy?). Having changed their state whilst maintaining rapport, there is more chance of successful communication.

You will only find out how powerful these techniques are by trying them. It is happening all the time, and naturally good communicators apply these simple principles without realising it. But because we are not aware of the phenomenon we do not consciously use mirroring as a communication skill. Initially, pacing and leading will feel unnatural and contrived, but with practice it will become an unconscious and very effective skill.

Applications for managers

There are plenty of applications for managers. Here are some situations in which you can try out the techniques.

- *Putting a nervous interview candidate at ease.*   Start by pacing their behaviour partially at least, then gradually opening your own behaviour as you lead them into a more relaxed state.
- *Pacifying an angry boss or colleague.*   Different people have different ways of expressing their anger, so your aim should be to lead them into a *different* behaviour by pacing and leading. Some people, for instance, tend to speak slowly and quietly when they are upset or angry, so this would be your starting pace. In this case you would lead by increasing the volume of your speech and speeding it up rather than the other way round. *You* establish and maintain

rapport by pacing, and *you* decide when and how to lead, taking as your cue each incremental matching of behaviour on their part. *You* have control over the communication and its outcome.

- **Persuading a colleague or client who is sceptical.** Top salespeople get amazing results through these techniques, which often seem to have a greater impact in the outcome of the communication than the strength of the actual argument or the objective quality of the product or service being sold. Physiological mirroring creates trust.

- **Getting a person who is taking an issue light- heartedly to treat it more seriously.** Facial expression is important in all these cases, and can help communicate the mood in which a communication is made. And you can maintain rapport, which is more to do with 'likeness' than whether a communication is formal or relaxed.

- **Introduce humour into a situation.** If a conversation seems too formal or a bit heavy, you can pace and lead towards a less formal and more easygoing atmosphere; often light humour, with congruent body language, is the most effective way.

- **Bringing a meeting to order, or to a close, or persuading a group on an important matter.** Applying these techniques will obviously be different in a group situation, as you will have to respond to different points of view, feelings and associated body language. In reality, however, a whole audience can be led by a powerful communicator, so you should certainly be able to use the technique with a small group. Often only one or a couple of people have to be convinced, so that in practice your mirroring actions can be directed to those who have the most influence, are the key decision-makers, or are otherwise central to the success of the communication.

- **Getting someone enthusiastic who is lethargic.** Remember that it is a natural tendency for us to mirror physiology, so it is no surprise that we talk about enthusiasm as being infectious.

- **Getting a change of state.** A slight mismatch can be enough to break the other person's state, and get more attention, without breaking rapport. Almost any gesture which is not expected will tend to bring a person quickly to the here and now, and you can get across an important point in your message. Even a couple of seconds break in the flow of conversation or a drop in the volume of your voice will fulfil this state change.

- *Summarily ending a communication.* A bigger mismatch, such as standing up or turning away, or clapping the palms of your hands on the desk, will break rapport. If this is your outcome, it is a highly effective technique. Looking over the other person's shoulder at a party, although a little more subtle, has a similar effect, although it might take a couple of minutes longer.

CONGRUENCE

It is unlikely, of course, that you will be able to generate enthusiasm in others if you are not really enthusiastic yourself. And this introduces the important principle of congruence. In our communication there has to be a match between the words we use and the accompanying characteristics such as physiology and voice tone. Our ability to detect people who are insincere, although often put down to a sixth sense or intuition, is likely to be based on our unconscious interpretation of the congruency of the communication. In extreme cases people actually shake their heads when making a positive point – denoting 'no', but quite unknowingly. Similarly 'closed' body language like tightly crossed legs and folded arms, or perhaps losing eye contact, might well indicate incongruence with words which suggest acceptance of what you are saying. So congruence *within* a person is just as important for communication as congruence between people, as illustrated by matching. You cannot always directly influence congruence in another person, and may not be aware, for instance, of the unconscious intentions that are at work. But you can take responsibility for your own part of the communication, which is to establish and maintain rapport. You can also become skilled at detecting and calibrating both rapport and congruence. And you can help by being congruent yourself.

Heart and mind

The need for congruence crops up repeatedly in NLP, reflecting not least the fact that we tend to have many parts to our personality, and thus do not necessarily think and act in a coherent, unequivocal way. The difference often expressed as between 'heart and mind' may simply reflect the way our respective two brains – right and left – operate: logically on the one hand, and holistically and intuitively on the other. Other differences may reflect the different intentions we pursue, consciously and unconsciously, which may be in conflict, and which was covered when we considered the ecology involved in setting outcomes.

Incongruence in action

Consider in each of the above examples of applications for managers the extent to which incongruence may play a part. A manager might go through the motions of setting an interview candidate at ease, while at the same time – perhaps less consciously – enjoying the impression of status and power he is communicating. The latter 'communication' might be the dominant one perceived by the interviewee, who might not be impressed, so the manager fails in both his outcomes. Whatever your words and conscious behaviour, scores of signals, in your voice, eye movements and body language, will betray your real intentions. If these are at odds with your conscious message, there is likely to be incongruent, ineffective communication.

Real and hidden agendas

Similarly you may have no real desire to pacify an angry colleague, although you perhaps go through the motions, but would prefer rather to 'give as good as you get', asserting your own point of view. Once again, it is unlikely that either of your outcomes - in effect your real and hidden agendas – will be fulfilled. Your incongruent behaviour is more likely to achieve neither. That is, you will fail to pacify the person, and certainly win no arguments. As well as failing in your immediate outcome, incongruent behaviour might actually be counter-productive in terms of long-term relationships.

Incongruence and customer care

In these enlightened days of 'the customer is king' there can also be incongruence when dealing with customers, clients, suppliers and other outsiders, besides work colleagues. Many companies have realised that expensive customer care training and impressive mission statements are a waste of money if behaviour at the coal face is not congruent. Customers usually sense when a script or standard body language is being followed, and once again the effect is counterproductive. Customer care starts with attitudes, values and beliefs – about the company and product, for instance, which result in *naturally* congruent behaviour. And that's the secret: when you get your ecology and outcomes right, the communication will be natural and uncontrived, and more effective.

We discussed earlier the common theme of likeness. We tend to like people who are like us, and communicate with them better. This is illustrated in the almost magical effectiveness of pacing and leading techniques. These are simple techniques, and you can start applying them immediately. But they can be developed to an extraordinary level of skill, so the search for excellent communication is an ongoing one. 'Likeness' applies in other than physiological ways, too. We may *think* like the other person, have similar interests to them, or have similar attitudes, values and beliefs. 'She's my kind of person', or 'We are on the same wavelength' are the expressions we hear, which almost guarantee good communication. Having described some behavioural ways to improve your communication, in the remainder of this part of the book I will introduce some of these 'neuro' aspects of NLP which so affect communication.

9

Using Your Senses

YOU can be like the other person in the way you *think* as well as in the way you appear outwardly or behave. For example, some people are optimists and others pessimists. Some seem to have 'tidy minds' and others seem to be disorganised, inwardly as well as outwardly. Then one person seems to think in pictures, while another runs internal dialogue, or self-talk, and yet another person has to *feel* right about everything. This chapter is concerned with how we prefer to think, or represent things – in pictures, sounds, or feelings, or internal dialogue. This is a major factor in communication – it is a fundamental way in which some people are alike, and others different, and so affects rapport.

According to the NLP model, we think by representing experience – sights, sounds, feelings, tastes, smells – inwardly. For example you can think about an event in the past by recalling the images, sounds and feelings it evokes, but you can just as easily imagine the future using the same 'representation systems'. These are the five senses, referred to as visual, auditory, kinaesthetic, gustatory (taste) and olfactory (smell). Each representation system is termed a *modality*, and the characteristics or qualities of the systems are termed *submodalities*. Examples of visual submodalities are brightness and focus, and auditory submodalities include volume and pitch – just as when adjusting a television. We shall meet more of these submodalities, which illustrate just how rich and unique are our individual ways of representing the world around us.

The importance of these modalities in communication is that they are the systems we use to form our maps of the world. So, in communicating, we can base our understanding of how the *other* person thinks and feels on a model of the five senses and their submodalities. What do *they* see, hear and feel inside? But each of us usually has a *preference* – to 'think' in images or sounds, for instance. This preference might be just marginal – we are a bit more at home with feelings, say, than sounds. Or it may be quite dominant, in which case we have difficulty understanding how anyone can think differently. It so happens that, collectively, we use the visual sense most, followed by auditory, then by kinaesthetic. The olfactory and gustatory senses, although very significant in certain memory recall situations, do not figure highly in everyday thought processing, and are consequently not such a big factor in communication. We have already seen the importance of 'likeness' in communication. Having the same thinking, or sensory preference also tends to enhance rapport.

SENSORY PREFERENCE

By getting to know the thinking preference of the person you are communicating with, and changing your behaviour to literally make more sense to them, you can increase rapport. Surprisingly, it is not difficult to do this. One give-away is the words, or *predicates*, we instinctively use. A visual person might refer to having 'a clear picture', or remark 'I see what you mean', while an auditory person will use phrases like 'I hear what you say' or 'that sounds fine'. Once you are aware of the tendency to prefer a way of thinking, you will start to notice these predicates all the time in conversation as well as when reading newspapers, reports, or letters. Here is a list of some which will already be familiar.

- *Visual.* 'I see what you mean', 'a blind spot', 'it appears', 'you'll look back on this', 'show me', 'eye to eye', 'mind's eye', 'sight for sore eyes', 'looking closely', 'hazy notion', 'shed some light'.
- *Auditory.* 'In a manner of speaking', 'turn a deaf ear', 'rings a bell', 'word for word', 'loud and clear', 'on the same wavelength', 'unheard-of', 'calling the tune', 'makes him/her tick'.
- *Kinaesthetic.* 'Hold on a second', 'cool customer', 'warm-hearted person', 'thick-skinned', 'I can grasp that

idea', 'heated argument', 'smooth operator', 'I can't put my finger on it', 'scratch the surface', 'I feel it in my bones', 'I will be in touch', 'turns me on'.

- **Olfactory and gustatory.** 'Smell a rat', 'bitter pill', 'fresh as a daisy', 'acid comment', 'that will go down well', 'swallow that', 'matter of taste', 'one man's meat'.

Non-verbal sensory cues

As well as the words we use, our body language and voice characteristics also reflect our preference, or the way we happen to be thinking at the time. A strongly visual person tends to speak quickly, in a high pitch and with shallow breathing. An auditory person will probably speak more slowly and resonantly, and might well adopt rhythmic body movements such as tapping a pen or moving the foot. He or she is likely to adopt a natural listening posture, with the head attentively to one side. A kinaesthetic person is more likely to speak slowly and ponderously, breathe slowly, and perhaps look down – feeling, rather than seeing or hearing, what is going on inside before making a reply. Once you are aware of these non-verbal cues you will be in an even better position to know the sensory preference of your colleagues and those you communicate with. You can then start to incorporate them into your matching behaviour, thus further increasing rapport.

Eye access cues

Another way to identify a person's thinking preference is by their eye movements. We tend to move our eyes according to which representation system we are accessing. In most cases this is a reliable indicator of how the person is thinking – often more reliable than the words they say. Upward eye movements indicate visual thought processes, and auditory processes involve looking sideways. Downward eye movements usually denote either kinaesthetic sensing, or internal dialogue, sometimes referred to as self-talk. These eye movements also differ as between memories recalled and constructed sounds and images, such as when imagining a scenario in the future that you have not experienced before.

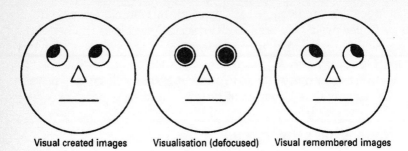

Visual created images **Visualisation (defocused)** **Visual remembered images**

Created sounds

Remembered sounds

Feelings and bodily
sensations

Internal dialogue

FIGURE 7 Eye access cues

These movements have been tested in extensive research, but you can quickly test them for yourself just as with the verbal and physiological clues we have already met. You can add these to your own observation of sensory preferences. This will require more skill than listening for familiar sensory words, or watching for major differences in body language. Sometimes the eyes move quickly, and several different representations are involved, although one may be dominant. So do your practising one stage at a time, watching out for eye movements exclusively one day, for example, and listening for verbal predicates on another.

When you are familiar with these preferences, and the actual preference of those you communicate with, the words they tend to use will make more sense. The sensory predicate 'I see what you are saying', although the term is used frequently, makes little sense until you are aware that the other person thinks in a visual way. Similarly, how can a picture of the new plant 'feel right', or even 'sound great', until you are aware of the variety of structure of thought and different sensory maps of reality.

Applications for managers

You can do several things to establish the thinking preference of people you regularly communicate with.

- Listen for the above predicates, or others that suggest one of the three main modalities – seeing, hearing, feeling – in everyday conversation. See whether one predominates, or perhaps two. Notice conversely the absence of predicates you or others use readily.
- Get hold of a report or similar piece that the person has written and check through for predicates in the same way. We tend to use these in writing as well as in speech, reflecting the way we mentally represent things all the time.
- Start using predicates, in spoken conversation and written communications, to match known preferences, and notice the difference it makes. You will probably find that talking to a kinaesthetic person in terms of 'grasping the subject' or 'feeling uneasy about something' creates far more rapport,

when previously you may have had difficulty getting through
to the person.
- Observe the non-verbal behaviour characteristics and eye
  access cues as further clues to preference.
- Bear in mind the person's sensory preference when
  submitting a report, writing a memo (using appropriate
  sensory predicates), giving a presentation, or communicating in any other way to a boss, colleague or client.

It always helps communication when you move towards the
other person's way of seeing things, and this onus is on the
communicator, who can use the appropriate sensory predicates and communication aids. But you can also lead the other
person to adopt a *different* modality, so that they too see things
(or hear or feel them) in a different way. This can often
unblock a communication. 'How would you picture so-and-so'
or 'how would you feel about it', although instinctively the
wrong language for a kinaesthetic or visual person respectively,
can be asked in an incremental pacing and leading way. We all
use all our senses inwardly – we simply have preferences. Using
a different representation system helps you see things in a
different light.

Identifying your own thinking preference

You may already be aware of your own thinking preference; for
instance, whether you tend to think in pictures and can easily
visualise different future scenarios, or whether you engage in a
lot of inner dialogue, listening to yourself giving encour-
agement or reprimands. On the other hand these are not
always a conscious part of our thinking, in the way we might
work out a multiplication or solve a word puzzle. At the same
time we are not usually aware of the predicates we use even
frequently, even though others may be, and we are certainly
not conscious of all the body language which reflects our inner
representations. You can now start to identify your own
preference, if you have one, and the following simple test might
help. This is far from scientific, but if the result you get shows
a strong bias, the chances are it would hold up in a more
sophisticated psychometric test.

The following simple exercises are taken from my book *NLP: The New Art and Science of Getting What You Want*. All you have to do is assess how easy or hard it is for you to internally represent each situation or experience. For instance, if a thought is very clear and focused – almost as real as in real life – you should score high on the subjective score chart. On the scale of 1 to 9, in the case just mentioned you would give yourself a nine. If you have difficulty getting any clear image, or it is transient, a score of one or two is more appropriate. And so on for sounds and feelings. If you are honest and consistent in your instinctive scoring, you will finish up with your likely preference.

Visual

1. Which of your friends or relatives has the longest hair?
2. Recall the face of a teacher from when you were at school.
3. Visualise the stripes on a tiger.
4. See the colour of the front door where you live or work.
5. See a favourite entertainer on your TV screen wearing a top hat.
6. Visualise the largest book in your house.

Auditory

1. Hear a favourite tune.
2. Listen to church bells ringing in the distance.
3. Which of you friends has the quietest voice?
4. Hear a car engine starting on a cold morning.
5. Imagine hearing the voice of a childhood friend.
6. Listen to the sound your voice makes under water.

Kinaesthetic

1. Feel your left hand in very cold water.
2. Hold a smooth, glass paperweight in both hands.
3. Stroke a cat or dog.
4. Put on a pair of wet socks.
5. Imagine jumping off a four-foot-high wall.
6. Roll a car wheel down the road.

Visual

1.	1	2	3	4	5	6	7	8	9
2.	1	2	3	4	5	6	7	8	9
3.	1	2	3	4	5	6	7	8	9
4.	1	2	3	4	5	6	7	8	9
5.	1	2	3	4	5	6	7	8	9
6.	1	2	3	4	5	6	7	8	9

Auditory

1.	1	2	3	4	5	6	7	8	9
2.	1	2	3	4	5	6	7	8	9
3.	1	2	3	4	5	6	7	8	9
4.	1	2	3	4	5	6	7	8	9
5.	1	2	3	4	5	6	7	8	9
6.	1	2	3	4	5	6	7	8	9

Kinaesthetic

1.	1	2	3	4	5	6	7	8	9
2.	1	2	3	4	5	6	7	8	9
3.	1	2	3	4	5	6	7	8	9
4.	1	2	3	4	5	6	7	8	9
5.	1	2	3	4	5	6	7	8	9
6.	1	2	3	4	5	6	7	8	9

Now add up your total score for each of the three modalities and divide by six to work out an average for each modality. Notice whether one of the three categories gives you a higher score than the other two, or whether one is significantly lower than the other two. If you want to make your preference score more accurate – although it is just a subjective measure – you can think of some more examples yourself. You might also want to break down the scoring into memory (recalling) and more imaginative (constructive) thoughts, to further isolate your preference.

If you find you have no particular preference but your scores are generally low, then practice will help, just as with any physical skill, and will prove useful in later exercises that will be of specific benefit. If, on the other hand, your scores are all high, you have a good foundation upon which to base a whole range of mental exercises that can improve your performance in any area you wish. At the very worst, your new knowledge about yourself should make you more aware of differences from person to person, and where vital rapport might be lacking.

USING SENSORY INTELLIGENCE

You should now be able to identify your own thinking preference, and that of those you frequently communicate with. This is valuable intelligence for any manager. Using the principle of rapport, and the flexibility we met in the four-part success cycle, you will be able to adjust your behaviour to improve your hit rate of successful communication.

Consider the sort of difficulties encountered by people of different preference. Trying to communicate to a visual person by carefully chosen words and well-articulated spoken arguments is unlikely to have the effect you want. But a couple of well-chosen illustrations, or even a few scribbles on a flip chart to make a point, can work wonders. Your words will have to back up the visual approach, so you may need to paint word pictures that make it easy for them to *see* what you are talking about. Use visual predicates like 'see', 'clear', 'focus', or 'imagine', which will be comfortable to your visual colleague.

Conversely, an auditory person will not be impressed by pictures – 'just *tell* me, spell it out in simple language' may be their reaction to a visual presentation. A kinaesthetic person may not be content until they have touched and felt something to support the communication. They will want to handle the actual product, for instance, or physically try out a process 'hands on'. The glossiest pictures may have little effect, but sit them in the driver's seat, let them *feel* the quality, and their senses will be turned on. With the right sensory language and aids, your kinaesthetic colleagues will 'grasp the argument', 'get a handle on the subject', and 'have a better feel for the proposition'. In each case, predicates and body language will need to support the actual medium of your communication, to reinforce the likeness and rapport you are trying to establish. So your personal sensory 'intelligence' about clients and fellow workers, and simple rapport-building skills, can be translated into sales, convincing presentations, or successful negotiations – anything that demands state-of-the-art communication.

Mismatching among managers

Now that you are aware of sensory differences, you might well recall instances of mismatched thinking preference in different management situations. Something that is obvious to you may be less so when you try to convince your boss, or a manager in another function. Typically the frustrated reaction is 'he just can't see it' or 'she doesn't seem to listen' or 'he just could not grasp what my department feels'. A carefully prepared report can be summarily thrown out if you are not aware of this simple principle of communication and neurological fact. It may take a little time to acquire the skill of thinking synaes-thetically – being able to switch easily between different modalities. Meanwhile, just behaving in a way that matches the other person and increases rapport, will produce successful communication outcomes. Another bonus is the better relationships you will establish over the longer term. By adopting such behaviour and increasing your sensory skills, you will also enrich your own thinking powers, and be more able to create strong internal goals.

First impressions

Mismatching crops up in all sorts of situations. An apparent poor 'first impression' gained from an interviewee, customer, or new member of staff may be simply a matter of a mismatch of sensory preference. It is almost as though you are speaking different languages. The communication presupposition puts the onus on the communicator to fulfil an outcome. You can't blame the person who didn't see, hear or feel; their way of perceiving the world is as legitimate as your own, and, they would no doubt consider, serves them well. This is all part of understanding each other's maps, and of making our respective maps of reality more rich and useful.

Using sensory preference as a communication tool involves the sensory acuity we discussed at the beginning of the book, and the ability to spot the signs of another way of thinking. It also demands flexibility to change our own behaviour in a way that will bring about a better transfer of understanding, and consequently the fulfilment of our outcome. An understanding of sensory preference, and the skill to recognise and adapt to differences, is thus a vital part of successful communication and personal achievement. In the next chapter I examine other ways in which we are like or unlike the people we communicate with. By understanding and bridging these differences we can find opportunities to communicate better and achieve more.

10

Understanding Each Other's Strategies

IN addition to having our own overall sensory thinking preferences, we also each have different thinking strategies or programs that apply to our behaviour at different levels. For instance, regardless of the modality we favour, one person may be generally optimistic and another pessimistic. Whilst each interprets the same outside reality, be it an electricity bill, clouds gathering in the distance, or a proposed reorganisation of the business, a different *strategy* is employed. Even two visualisers who might otherwise have related well, comparing their vivid mind pictures, might not enjoy rapport if one is an inveterate worrier and the other the eternal optimist. Both use their mental skills to the full in their own way, but adopt very different strategies.

Meta programs

A whole approach to work, or to life generally, which involves being optimistic, or receptive, for instance, is an example of a high-level macro strategy, or meta program. The word meta comes from the Greek and means beyond or above, or on a different level. These tend to embrace large chunks of lower-level behaviour – right down to how you interpret a passing comment from the boss, how you word a letter, or how you spend your time. We all have well-entrenched mental programs which automatically filter our experience, and govern all our behaviour, accounting for the dramatic differences in temperament and behaviour from person to person. Meta programs are described as being 'content-free' – it doesn't matter whether we are concerned about the monthly accounts,

Freda's birthday, or a bowls tournament. Whatever the actual situation or event, we filter our experience according to well-established personal patterns.

Matching such strategies will enhance rapport in the same way that other perceived likeness does. Two worriers will have a great time with their mutual lamentations, and an optimistic entrepreneur, academic, or social reformer will relate best to people with similar ways of thinking. (Common interests, of course, might mean lively arguments, but this is often a sign of healthy rapport.) So communication can also be helped by understanding and where possible, responding to these strategies. How often has a strained conversation suddenly come to life when some common ground is discovered? So the communication bottom line is to get to know the main thinking strategies, or meta programs, of the other person. This is his or her map of reality, and it is this map you are getting into in any communication.

There are other examples of meta programs which I will now discuss.

Pleasure or pain

We all act in a way that seeks to increase pleasure or decrease pain. We have different perceptions of these, of course, and one person will delight in what another abhors. But some have a greater tendency to move *towards* something they want, while others are more likely to move *away from* things they don't want. Each 'driver' can be highly motivating, and bring similar results, although positive motivation tends to be stronger.

One person describes what they want, and another person describes what they don't want. One person will eventually get out of bed because of the fear of what terrible things will happen if they don't turn up for work, or whatever. Another person gets out of bed motivated by something pleasurable, however innocuous, that the day holds in store. One person will plan for their retirement to avoid the horrors of financial dependence and loneliness, while another, in a similar job and family situation, will look forward positively to the new pleasures that retirement promises. One person might respond to 'if you don't . . .', while another will respond to 'if you do . . .'. In some cases the absence of pain is as good as pleasure, while others demand something much more positive and fulfilling.

This and other all-embracing strategies are built upon our unique and varied experience, and in particular our early environment and the values and attitudes to which we were subject in early life. Of course, there are exceptions. In some situations we might be motivated away from pain, when normally we are positively motivated, or vice versa, depending on the context. But generally we have a dominant tendency one way or the other. And people with the same dominant tendency tend to enjoy rapport and to communicate well.

Inner or outer recognition

We also tend to be motivated by rewards of different sorts. But whereas one person will be satisfied with having done a good job, measuring up to their own inner standard of success, another will need external recognition. This might involve actual rewards, such as financial, or spoken or written praise and recognition. One criterion for judging behaviour is internal, and the other is external.

A person with an internal frame of reference will do well in a job involving little contact with others, monitoring, or tangible outputs. He or she usually 'knows inside', without having to check everything out with others, or may just 'feel something is right'. Another person might require daily 'stroking', however innocuous, to maintain their goal orientation. All sorts of recognition symbols like certificates, 'salesperson of the month' awards, and regular staff appraisals are based on the importance to many people of external criteria of success. It is less widely appreciated that those who are internally motivated respond to different criteria, and may for instance be able to take on far more responsibility without detailed supervision, or carry out important projects that do not have short-term or tangible outcomes. Maybe the odd 'well done' is all they need.

Higher up the management hierarchy it is more important to be internally driven, as external praise may be thin on the ground, and bold decisions have to be made without complete data. People with an external frame of reference respond to testimonials or name-dropping, but this will have little impact on an internally driven person.

Applications for managers

You may be able to identify the internal/external strategy of your boss, colleagues and subordinates. Having done so, you will be able to improve any communication by adjusting your behaviour and words to press their 'hot button'. The briefest 'thank you' will often suffice as outside recognition, and the fact, say, that several other departments, or a rival company (outside criteria) have already adopted a particular policy that is under consideration will be given a lot of weight. In some cases, recognition will need to be public or involve tangible trappings. On the other hand, lavish recognition, and especially the more overt rewards of public incentive systems, may actually be counterproductive with the kind of person whose rewards are intrinsic, and who just wants a worthwhile and demanding job to do in the first place.

These strategies are not fixed, and we might act differently depending on the context. For instance in a new post a manager might adopt a more external frame, whereas with long experience and confidence he or she may be more internally driven. But again, a dominant strategy is usually evident. Once you have identified a person's internal/external frame of reference, incentives become both more effective and may cost little or nothing to implement. If you know that Bob needs regular 'stroking', decide on a simple and consistent stroking strategy. Powerful, personal hot buttons are there for the pressing. If Gill needs lots of satisfaction and challenge in her work, make sure her tasks live up to this, if necessary agreeing from the outset the degree of monitoring, project milestones, and discretion expected. Then let her get on with it.

Matching and mismatching

Some people sort in terms of what things have in common, whilst others notice what is different. One person, for example, will spot a common trend, while the other notices an exception. A matcher will tend to generalise. A mismatcher usually focuses on specifics. On the occasions when you just do not hit it off with a person, the reason might be in this fundamental way in which each of you sees the world. If you don't recognise these meta programs for what they are, you can too easily write off a person as ignorant, belligerent, negative or nit-picking. What you have met with, in fact, is just another way of representing the world – another perceptual map – possibly equally valid to your own, and which is as likely to be as rich as it is unique.

Possibility or necessity

Some people are motivated by what is *necessary*, rather than by what is *possible*. They do things because they have to, rather than because they want to or see the possibilities in a course of action. Others are open to new possibilities and choices, and welcome the unknown. Each has very different behaviours regarding loyalty, risk-taking, compliance with rules and so on. Each has strengths to offer in different kinds of jobs or situations. You will probably expect an auditor or quality controller, or perhaps an airline pilot, to do what must be done and stick to the rule book. A more creative job or leadership role, on the other hand, will demand a mind that is open to new possibilities. Although mismatches of this sort can present obstacles in one-to-one communication, in a team problem-solving mode they actually provide welcome synergy – again provided they are recognised and valued for what they are: different thinking programs.

Style

We all have different styles of working. One person likes to operate independently, while another likes to work closely with others, cooperatively. These are further operating programs that we feel comfortable with, but which may not make sense to a person who has adopted a different strategy.

THE TIME DIMENSION

Another major difference between people is in the way they relate to time. Some people dwell on the past, others on the future, and others seem to live only for the present. A highly goal-oriented person who has clear objectives will usually think a lot in terms of where they are going, and the sort of experiences that will result. A visual person in particular will 'see' an experience in advance of it happening, so that it almost becomes the reality. But in a very similar way another person will be able to recall memories so vividly that in effect they carry their past around with them, which influences every current behaviour. In management, such a person would be less able to cope with change, or to grasp opportunities.

'Through time' and 'in time'

There are even cultural differences in our approach to time, in that western people tend to have a linear perception of time as if going through it, whereas a more Arabic concept of time is that of a perpetual present, and the past is behind. These differences in our individual so-called 'timelines' are reflected neurologically in the way we represent memories and future events. On the one hand, imagery of both past and present is ahead of us, just as with external vision. Typically, the past will be on one side and the future on the other, and this is referred to as 'through time'. The second type of person represents time as going from front to back, usually with the past behind, and some part of time actually 'inside'. So in this case you would have to turn your head to see a memory from the past. This type is referred to as 'in time' – part of the 'timeline' is inside you. As with other mental strategies, it is always hard to understand how someone thinks differently from yourself.

These ways of perceiving time offer further scope for differences, with resulting communication hazards. Subjectively, we can do all sorts of tricks with time. When we fall asleep time stands still, and our next conscious experience of time may be many hours later. Something similar happens when we daydream, or are lost in our own thoughts – in the state termed 'downtime'. Conversely, when we are highly focused on present reality we have a better awareness of the passing of time. Time can drag or fly, depending on what we are doing, and our experience of it changes constantly. And although we each experience time in these different ways, we nevertheless have our own familiar concepts and experience of time. One manager 'never turns up on time', while another 'has never been late in her life'. We all know of these differences, and what happens when such people try to relate and communicate.

Your personal timeline

Fortunately, our brains are able to take reasonable account of time. Thus you will be able to differentiate between a regular activity you carried out this morning, and the same one five years ago, and for that matter imagining doing the activity at some time in the future. In giving us a structure of thought processes, NLP can help in identifying the actual neurological differences that give us this instinctive awareness of time. By imagining similar past and present events or experiences, for example, you should be able to spot differences in the modalities (seeing, hearing, feeling) and submodalities ('picture' contrast and brightness, voice tone, etc.). This includes the *location* of the image, which as we have seen might differ as between left and right, or front and behind, when we represent time. In every thought, we represent not just experience, but the time dimension as well. The differences may be subtle, and sometimes we are not sure whether we have actually done something or just have imagined it clearly. The unique characteristics of how you sort out time represent your personal 'timeline'.

Time perception and communication

For present purposes we need to understand that others may not perceive time as we do, and our communication might thus be ineffective. As with sensory preference, our words can sometimes give clues. Phrases like 'I can't see any future' or 'I'm looking forward to the meeting' may be more literal than we might imagine. Similarly 'looking back on it' illustrates exactly how a past event is represented as such.

The biggest difference is likely to occur as between a 'through time' person and an 'in time' person, and this happens most when communicating across cultures. What may not be understood by most managers is that 'African time', or 'Arab time', reflect structurally different ways of representing time – it happens in the brain. But even 'through time' people may have different ways of perceiving time. In one case the past might be dim, small and less focused than the future, or vice versa, and this accounts for the different degrees of emphasis we each give to the present, past and future. A clear representation of both past and future will usually mean a person is very time conscious, and – for instance – they will be reliable timekeepers. A person whose timeline is less distinct will live more in the present, and may easily overlook appointments, or simply not appreciate the importance of keeping to time schedules. These difference happen in the brain as learned strategies involving actual electro-chemical processes.

In the case of colleagues you work with closely, you will no doubt be able to categorise them by experience. Do they seem to dwell in the past, think mainly about the future, or live for the present? How do they see the future? Clear and positive, or hazy and menacing? How do they represent their distant past, or an incident a couple of days ago? How real are past and future representations, and how do they motivate the person today? You will be in a position to understand the other person better by appreciating their different strategy for representing time – their different map of the world. You can then start using appropriate language, just as when matching their basic sensory (seeing, hearing, feeling) preference. At worst, your own feelings about apparently ineffective communications will be changed; you will be more aware of the different perceptions involved, and will have the choice to change your own behaviour to bring about a better outcome.

All this has immediate application for managers. You don't describe vivid future scenarios to a person who (effectively) has no future timeline to speak of. Nor would the short term delights of the present mean much to the person whose whole life seems to be a preparation for some future outcome or other.

The time dimension is, I found, a major factor in leadership. The orthodox role of leadership usually includes creating a vision. But many would-be leaders have difficulty communicating their vision of the future to colleagues, who may neither think visually nor have a strong future timeline. However, by matching meta programs as well as sensory preference, rapport can be established with uncanny ease.

Timescale and achieving goals

One of the most important factors in management and business generally concerns whether we act with short-term or long-term outcomes in mind. Timescale is a dimension which has to be brought into every goal-setting exercise, and usually there are trade-offs – we forfeit long-term benefits in return for early winnings, or we gain long-term advantage by bearing some cost in the short term. Insofar as these factors can be measured, or even identified, they will hopefully be part of any decision process. But our individual perception of time and its importance is bound to be a factor. A person who does not 'see' a long-term future is unlikely to give the same weight to long-term criteria as the person who seems to live for future expectations. A person who lives mainly in the present will be attracted to immediate or short-term outcomes, regardless of the economic or other logical sense. They just can't (or don't) *represent* a distant future in their minds. Most decisions involve judgement in any event, and the time dimension is simply another subjective basis for any such judgement, and a reflection of an individual map of reality. You should consider all of the following factors in terms of achieving your outcome in any communication.

- How will your outcome – especially the time dimension – 'make sense' to the other person?
- Is there an *angle* that will accommodate the other person's perception of the time factor? A future advantage, present benefit, or past experience?
- If you viewed time in the way that they do, what would motivate you? And what sort of communication would be effective for you?
- Can longer-term benefits be converted into a more tangible, present-day form? For example, long-term insurance benefits can give present-day peace of mind; a long project can give day-to-day job satisfaction if planned with frequent milestones and interim success criteria. Can you communicate a longer-term outcome in vivid, sensory terms?
- How can your actual language in the communication fit the other person's time perception? Do you use the term 'in the long run' or 'in the future', and does it make the same

'sense' to the person you are communicating with?

- Or can you amend your outcome but make it more likely to be achieved? Are there other ways to achieve the ultimate goal that have different time implications? How is your own idea of time, and its importance or lack of importance, built into your outcome and the way you describe it?

- How do you choose a person to do a long-term project with even longer-term outcomes? Is their 'timeline' a factor? Have they a track record of achieving over such a period? If a team is involved, how is it made up, in terms of different individual personal timelines? Are long-term goals and immediate action and responsiveness catered for?

- Consider what 'urgent' means, or 'ASAP' (as soon as possible), or 'immediately', to the person you are communicating with. Or 'few', as in 'a few days', 'a few weeks', or 'a few minutes'. Is there a better way of communicating what you want, to avoid misunderstanding and build on the other person's perception of time?

LIFE CONTENT

The Life Content model which we looked at earlier also comprises examples of meta programs. Many personality models identify people who are activists, or doers, as against those who are reflectors, or thinkers. One person acts before they think (if they get round to thinking), and another thinks before they act (if they ever get round to acting). These are examples of meta thinking styles, of which there are many. In the Life Content model, one person is acquisitive, concerned with *having* and *getting*, and attracted to the tangible evidence of success. Yet another person has to *know* everything about a behaviour – such as a hobby or a purchase they will make – before they embark on any action. Others are more concerned with relationships – what will so-and-so think, how will it affect the children, boss, neighbour, and so on. Yet another type of person is more concerned with their own identity, and how they feel. Rather than *doing* or *knowing* things, which may be secondary or interim aims, they want to *be* fulfilled, *be* happy, *be* a good manager, parent or whatever.

Like the tendency to need external recognition, or the tendency to be motivated towards rather than away from, these are types of human perceptive maps that we meet all the time. And on the basis that we have better rapport with people who are like us, we need to appreciate these different perspectives, some of which are bound to be unfamiliar or even strange to us – because *we are not like that*. All this prepares the ground for effective communication, and mastery in achieving our outcome. These strategies – doing, getting/having, knowing, relating, being – have a major effect on how we behave and how effectively we communicate. As with other NLP models, the Life Content model can help you understand yourself as well as other people. Both perspectives are needed for rapport and good communication.

Doing

A communication that is wholly designed to impart knowledge, when knowledge is not valued highly by the other person (at least on its own), is likely to fail. Conversely, a message aimed at bringing about action, even challenging, immediate action, might stand a better chance of success with a 'doing' person. A reflective, thinking person will usually distrust someone who goes feet first into everything, and vice versa. Communication between them will be strained and largely ineffective. But there is room for doers as well as thinkers, and even more room for managers who can appreciate the strengths of both and communicate to them in their own 'language'. As we have already seen, this places a lot of the onus on the communicator – often the manager who has to get a message across – or, more to the point, whoever wants to bring about an outcome through a communication.

But the burden need not be too heavy. Often these very different ways of seeing the world can be accommodated by minor changes, which will be more than rewarded by the success of your real outcome. Let's say you have a task to be done, which is ostensibly to gain knowledge or information. The chances are it will also include some *doing* – talking to people, visiting places, producing draft or interim reports, giving a presentation, making telephone calls, or whatever. All these are *activities*, and will appeal to a *doing* person. The secret is to portray the job in *doing* terms, that will make sense and appeal to the person. This may involve a slight change in the form and content of the job itself, but this may be cosmetic; the big change will be in how you communicate – the words you use and the mind pictures you create. Combined with an understanding of the person's sensory preference (which we covered in Chapter 9), you will be in a powerful position to achieve your outcome through people who otherwise you would not have got the necessary rapport with. All your team, all your staff, are thus harnessed into achieving the corporate goals you are trying to achieve, and that is what management is all about.

Having

Consider these Life Content differences in the case of a group doing a night school course to learn a language. One person wants to *do* the course. Another want to *know* the subject. Another wants to *relate* to the people both on the course and others whom they want to please or impress. Another wants to *be* a translator, and *be* financially independent of others. But another wants to *have* or *get* a certificate, putting a lot of value on the physical, tangible evidence of achievement. Each is motivated, but according to a different meta program. Their inner worlds are different, with different values and beliefs at work.

To a having/getting person in a work situation, the right paperweight, chair, or office size, along with money earnings, will probably be more important than the doing or knowing involved, or perhaps the relationships that are harmed in the 'getting' process.

In my research involving more than 150 top chairmen and chief executives I found extraordinary differences in the tangible trappings of office, which bore little relationship to company size or performance. These differences did reveal, however, stark contrasts in what was important to the people concerned, in terms of Life Content.

Having or *getting* hot buttons are just waiting to be pressed in return for any degree of motivation and commitment. There is usually little cost and effort involved when compared with the benefits involved – you just need to go to the bother of determining how the other person ticks, and adjust your communication so that it makes sense to them. Make sure they 'get' something, or have something to show for their effort. Respect their different dreams and priorities and start adjusting your 'language' to get your message across. 'Will you get hold of the Zeta report, get June's opinion, and let's have your one page proposal. Can you get this done by Friday?' The right Life Content language comes across as familiar and non-threatening, and of course gains vital rapport.

Knowing

Some people need to know, before doing or getting. They will read up all the brochures before booking a holiday, and study the instruction manual before daring to operate the equipment. In some cases the knowing seems to be an end in itself. Although part of any manager's job, it can become a major time-user. The *knowing* manager will usually spend a lot of time planning and weighing up the pros and cons of a decision, and gathering as much data as possible. He or she is less comfortable about doing things, and producing tangible results, especially on the basis of incomplete knowledge. You might recognise yourself in this description, or a close colleague or friend. The result can be that not much actually gets done. Fortunately, there are often complementary characteristics in other staff members which avoid the worst consequences for the organisation of any individual meta programs.

This macro thinking strategy is similar to the reflector or theorist styles that usually form part of a personality style profile. Communicating straight information to such a person may not present a problem, but if your communication outcome is action, or a tangible 'getting' result, your message needs to be specifically designed to achieve it. There are usually knowing aspects to a task or project as well as doing aspects, so it should be possible to emphasise these in a way that uses the strengths of the individual (all these specific personality traits can be a strength, in the right context), whilst achieving rapport by bridging to their mental map. The knowing person may not mind doing something to find out (to know) if it works, or getting something they perceive as requiring knowledge. 'You will need to know you have enough people, Charlie, so that the deadline will be met. You know what happened last time. We both need to be aware (knowledge) of anything that might affect performance. I am sure (I know) you will do what you know is needed.'

Similarly, the *doing* person may not mind getting to know enough to enable them to do something. So the way you communicate a task may mean the difference between success and failure – of *your* outcome. Flexibility, and maybe ingenuity and creativity, is called for, which is a more sensible communication strategy on your part than addressing someone in a language they don't understand, and expecting to get the right response.

Relating

This is akin to the need for external recognition we met earlier. When relationships are important, other people become the main criterion for behaviour. So, for instance, *getting* would be important to the extent of what someone, including the neighbours, might think about it, and the same might apply to *knowing* or *doing* – 'are the others doing it'; 'what will they think?'

At the highest level our thought patterns or strategies form what we term personality traits and basic attitudes. Interestingly, *relating* can also extend to a deceased relative we are, perhaps subconsciously, trying to please, or to a past mentor who has had an influence on our behaviour. More commonly, harmony in relationships – 'not rocking the boat' – whether at home or in the office, or the recognition of one or two respected or loved people, are the characteristics we would expect of a *relating* person. Getting on with the boss may thus be an overriding priority, affecting both day-to-day working and longer-term career. Or the desire for strong home relationships can similarly dictate other work behaviour. In some cases, a meta program to get a better job or bigger house may be serving just such a relating goal. All sorts of 'people' problems stem from these basic mental programs; the 'problems' are just as readily solved when the 'programs' are identified and we start to communicate in the right language.

Being

Although seeming to be a semantic distinction, there is a difference between *doing* a good job, and *being* a good manager; between succeeding and being successful; between *getting* something to make you happy and *being* happy. It has a lot to do with the timelines we met earlier; *being* is associated with the present. It is also more associated with personal identity and higher-level outcomes – like being content, or being fulfilled – than with lower level more specific ones like getting a salary increase or doing a night school course. In this case the project controller will respond to the need to *be* in control, *be* one step ahead, *be* on top of the paperwork, or *be* on time and on budget. 'Let's be clear, Valerie, we'll all be happy if you can pull this one off.'

As with sensory preference, we tend to prefer one Life Content strategy or the other. In practice we may be familiar with them all, but they have different orders of significance. More specifically, one is subsidiary to the other; for example, we may *do* in order to *get* in order to *be*. Or we may need to *know* in order to *relate*. There is likely to be an order, or syntax, to the way these behavioural strategies govern our lives. Knowing this personal syntax, as well as the dominant or preferred Life Content, means that you have important self-knowledge for your own part, and an effective hot button in communicating with others. Simply knowing that some people like to do first, then get to know, or get to know first then act, can enable you to communicate in those terms. Expressing a complete task or project in the right sequence of a person's Life Content profile is the way to communication excellence, and getting just what you want. For example: 'Find out so-and-so [knowing], do so-and-so, get this', makes sense to one person; 'Check with so-and-so [relating], then do so-and-so, to find out [knowing]' will be more comfortable to another. Remember that what seems strange or even illogical to you might be simple common sense to another person. As a manager, with a little creativity, you should be able to either structure tasks, or in some cases simply communicate them, in the way that fits the other person's Life Content map.

The tendency to action, knowledge, getting and having, or being may be as much to do with the culture of the organisation as any innate personality trait, and many managers do change their style, although not always consciously, when moving from job to job. But the implications in terms of communication are the same; a strategy, or way of thinking, controls behaviour. The person's map, of course, has changed, and they now represent things differently. Strategies are and can be changed, just as they often are when we move to another town, have a baby, or read an inspiring book.

IDENTIFYING META PROGRAMS

Meta programs are as varied as they are universal. You get to know them by watching, asking and listening. In most cases, particularly people you are in regular contact with, once you are aware of the main differences you will have no difficulty in spotting them – for instance, the person who seems to live in the past, or needs constant 'stroking', or who is concerned with material possessions and status symbols, or who has to understand all the implications of a task before they will get started. The words and expressions, or predicates, people use also betray the way their thoughts are structured, as we saw in recognising sensory preference.

You will need your 'sensory acuity' to get into the other person's 'map'. If you ask a person what they want out of a planned reorganisation or other proposal for change, or out of a relationship, do they tell you what they want or what they don't want? Do they describe a product or service in terms of what it saves you from (high fuel costs, accidents, ageing, etc.) or its positive benefits (speed, enjoyment, peace of mind). Do they talk in terms of how they feel or what other people might think or feel? Is their holiday experience all about places, or about doing things, or about people and relationships? Was their experience like a glass that is half-full or one that is half-empty? Do they talk of a present situation in terms of the past or in terms of the future? Do they speak of what *should* happen, or what *could* happen? Specific techniques will not provide the sensory acuity you need to elicit these tendencies – you just need to be aware of the main patterns and apply common sense. There is also skill involved, which comes with practice.

As with sensory preference, it may help if you do not attempt too much at one time. For instance, try spotting examples of only one of the above meta programs on a particular day. Alternatively, focus on one person (say in a meeting) rather than several. Just as when learning to drive a car or acquiring any complex skill, you need to learn in manageable chunks, until you can do everything at once without even realising you are doing it.

All manner of communication blockages can be related to differences in the way these meta programs operate from person to person. When you understand how the other person thinks – how they actually structure their perceptions in these very different ways – you will start to get into their map of reality. That is what communication is all about. Even a marginal understanding of these important strategies can be more crucial to an effective communication than the choice of medium or even the words of the message itself. 'Likeness' means rapport, and rapport means a better mutual under-standing. People with a good relationship hardly need to communicate at all in the formal sense that management textbooks often suggest.

Common interests, such as in sport, politics, or hobbies can also create rapport upon which communication can be based. And as well as so-called meta programs, we have lower level strategies that govern every aspect of our behaviour. There are strategies for spelling or remembering names, for mental arith-metic, or winning a job interview. There are strategies for squeezing out toothpaste, washing dishes, and office filing. They can be at one time either barriers to rapport and commu-nication, or the very key to excellent communication. NLP makes us aware of these factors, but also offers ways to change strategies so that they serve us better. Specific strategies for excellence are discussed in more detail in Part Four.

11

Getting Language on Your Side: The Meta Model

IT would be unusual to consider the subject of communication without thinking about language. The linguistic
element of NLP is implicit in the title. Good communicators
know how to use and abuse language to get what they want.
There are times, for instance when it helps to be precise: 'Let's
meet at the station', for example, might be spelled out more
clearly if you want to avoid any possible misunderstanding and
wasted time and effort all round. There are other times,
however, when it helps to be vague. If you want a member of
your staff to use their initiative and come up with creative
ideas, the less detail of the task you spell out, the better.
Similarly, allowing your customer's mind to freely wander
round the imagined, cosmic delights of a product or service
can be more effective than directing them to some technical
detail of the product specification. Non-specific language, or
metaphors without direct association, can stimulate the imagination and bridge mental maps, whereas detail and analysis,
even with the best intentions, can kill off rapport and true
communication – as unending minutes with a technically
genius sales assistant will prove. So language in communication is a matter of horses for courses – as ever, it comes back
to the outcome you want to achieve.

One of the early major models of NLP is known as the Meta
Model, and it concerns the way we use language, and how it
can help us to understand other people's mental maps. It is a

tool for understanding better what people mean by what they say, and is an example of using language to get more precise meaning. As with sensory preference, and the meta programs we have been learning about, this language model can help you to understand yourself as well as others, and especially in making issues, problems or outcomes clear. In this chapter I apply it to communication, but you will soon spot other ways you can use it, such as in problem solving or controlling how you feel.

Language, amazing though it is, is no more than an anaemic representation of the mass of rich thoughts we all experience and might want to communicate. Most of our language, however, is used at a surface level. For instance, you might say 'She had an accident'. The deeper meaning is that 'Shirley, a 38-year-old personal assistant with Gregory and Co. and mother of two children broke her arm just above the wrist when she fell . . .' and so on. More meaning could be added, *ad infinitum*. In other words, what we say with language is just a convenient potted representation of our knowledge and understanding.

This, of course, is the only way we can carry on reasonable social interaction, but it is fraught with problems for the unwary. The simplification process means that we:

- *generalise*, so that a lot of specific understanding is not transmitted;
- *omit* all kinds of information, which we assume the other person understands, or that we think insufficiently significant in terms of our communication; and
- *distort* meaning, whether knowingly or unknowingly.

Surface structure and deep structure

The Meta Model identifies common language patterns which are examples of all of these types of simplification. When we appreciate the structures of language – a *surface structure* used in everyday communication, and a *deep structure* involving all manner of thought patterns – it is not hard to understand how meaning can get lost or distorted. By identifying common language patterns that reflect these limitations, we can be ready to both spot and respond to any communication in a more informed, mindful way.

The model identifies a dozen common patterns covering the three language categories of generalisations, omissions and distortions. Most of these will be immediately familiar to managers, and others will 'ring a bell' as soon as examples are given. As this model is an important part of NLP and illustrates starkly the communication pitfalls managers continually meet, I will describe each one. Not surprisingly, this linguistic model comes with its own jargon, which I will – reluctantly – adopt, this hopefully being no more of an annoyance than we have suffered from computer, accountancy and other specialist fields.

Although language-based, the model has wider significance within NLP. What might be called the 'NLP model' involves the way we represent internally the five modalities of seeing, hearing, feeling, smelling and tasting. We have also seen the way the many stimuli that enter our brains are filtered according to our different values, beliefs and unique perceptions about what things mean. This filtration, although applying to all the senses, also seems to follow the Meta Model pattern: that is, we generalise, omit and distort information. So, as communication is all about getting understanding from one person's mind to another, we have to mutually negotiate these personal filters. Fortunately, language, with all its limitations, gives us some very useful clues as to how we each think, and the Meta Model is a powerful tool to do just that.

Try to keep in mind the questions listed in the first chapter. Not only will the model have a ring of truth, but you will think of ways you can use it to communicate better. Also, remember that in NLP you don't have either/or problems about principles, models and techniques – everything you have learned so far is still valid. Just because you get a fancy new drill for Christmas, you don't have to throw out your whole tool kit. So keep in mind the communication presuppositions (Chapter 3), and the whole world of non-verbal communication we covered in the earlier chapters of Part Three.

Generalisations

Universal quantifiers

Certain universal or absolute terms are almost guaranteed to raise emotions and wreck communication. Whether at the giving or receiving end, some words exact a high price in the end. 'You *always* say that', or 'You *never* do so-and-so', besides probably being untrue, do little to create the rapport upon which communication depends. They are usually supported, of course, by a deeper meaning that is left uncommunicated. What is *actually* communicated, however, may not be what you had intended, or what will best achieve your outcome. Other words that fall into this category are 'every', 'all' and 'none'. These can be deadly, leaving no room for give and take in dialogue, and suggest a mindset that says 'My map is the true map'. The *response* in this case is 'Always?', 'Never?', 'None of the time?' By re-presenting the generalising word as a question, you can usually expose the weakness of what is being said, and either explicitly or implicitly elicit a more specific meaning.

This pattern is usually easy to spot, because of the universal-type words that are used. Similarly, no special response needs to be remembered, other than a reversal of the offending pattern. However, sometimes universal quantifiers are more hidden. For example, 'Bosses are out for what they can get' implies that *all* bosses are, which is, to say the least, a generalisation. The response is the same: 'Do you mean *all* bosses?', although in this case you may easily miss the generalisation. Fortunately, with absolutes, you are on pretty safe ground assuming the statement to be untrue – there is always an exception. In this example, the deeper structure probably involves a couple of bosses who in the person's experience seemed to be out for what they could get, and an *opinion* that some or many others were like them.

Hidden universals, however, are not so easy to spot, especially as they come in the flow of conversation and you are concerned with the subject matter of the conversation, rather than the structure of the language pattern. 'The young ones are the worst', if it is to have the effect probably intended, implies all the young ones, and you can find yourself going along with such a sentiment without a thought of the 'territory' of reality.

By spotting the generalisation, you can choose how you treat such a surface-level statement, including whether you want to make any response. Note that the speaker may not have *meant* all, although he implied it. An appropriate response will quickly establish this. If he really meant all, he is on shaky ground and this might weaken any further communication based on that foundation. Again, you have the choice to 'take it with a pinch of salt', saying nothing, or to respond by exposing nonsense, prejudice, misunderstanding or whatever generalisation the statement contains. Or he didn't *mean* all, but intended to *communicate* all, to bring about a certain communication outcome (to persuade, impress, startle, or whatever). However you choose to respond, by recognising a Meta Model pattern you have choices and control over outcomes – including other people's – so practice and skill are rewarded.

Modal operators of possibility

The give-away words in this case are 'cannot', 'impossible', or 'possible'. Expressions like 'You can't do that' or 'That's impossible' are standard currency of managers. But these are just as likely to be generalisations as 'never' or 'always', with which they are often combined: 'I'll never manage that', implying the person can't. The response is to ask 'What, precisely, is stopping you?' Or 'What would happen if you did?' Or 'What would have to happen to make this possible?'

As well as being a barrier to communication, this language pattern is also damaging to achievement. It reflects a common self-fulfilling negative mindset. It also eliminates the choices – the different ways of seeing things or doing things – upon which, as we have seen, achieving outcomes depends.

Top managers and business people are uncannily united in promoting what is usually called a 'can-do' attitude: a positive attitude is worth months of management training.

These patterns illustrate how much our thinking and language are bound together, and the power of simple words in dictating outcomes.

Modal operators of necessity

The sister pattern is the modal operator of necessity, which is recognised by words like 'should', 'shouldn't', 'ought', 'must not', etc. These implicitly call on a higher authority, or some unseen rule book, and may hark back to educational and social conditioning in childhood. 'You shouldn't involve the so-and-so department' would get the response, 'What would happen if I did?' Note that a 'Why' response might raise ethical and other questions which would not move the communication forward. 'What' and 'How' questions seem to get more quickly to the deeper meaning.

NLP is not prescriptive – it offers the language pattern for a response, rather than how to use it. There is no substitute for flexibility and some ingenuity in eliciting precise meaning. Furthermore, your tone of voice and accompanying body language will have to be congruent if you are to maintain rapport while questioning what might be sensitive matters.

Complex equivalence

Sometimes two statements are put together to give the impression that they mean the same thing. For example: 'He must be annoyed . . . he was not sent a copy'. Or 'He's not interested . . . he never said a word.' In these cases 'not being sent a copy' is considered equivalent to 'being annoyed' and 'not saying a word' means 'you are not interested' – two plus two equalling five. Such statements are more difficult to identify than universal quantifiers and modal operators, which are usually associated with just a few specific words. They can work in a more sinister way, not always raising emotion yet changing real meaning by their generalisation. Once spotted, responding with the question 'How does this mean that?' should expose such statements for what they are. With a moment's reflection, it will be clear that these statements are not equivalent – exposure is usually all that is needed. Or a more precise communication will follow, in which case the Meta Model will have done its job.

Deletions

Unspecified nouns

'It annoys me'; 'They don't understand'. These common figures of speech omit the important noun so we need to know

'*What* annoys you?', or '*Who* doesn't understand?' A response can usually be got by asking 'Who or what specifically?' Apart from in everyday conversation, missing specific nouns are a feature of bureaucratic language, both spoken and written, in which managers often lead the field. A popular management style is to switch into passive mode so that 'Jane filled the job' or 'Fred drove the car', become 'The job was filled' and 'The car was driven'. This is a device for impersonalising matters which really have personal implications, and for being deliberately imprecise, as well as being a lazy form of communication. It often implies that you are not responsible for what is going on, but are a passive spectator. Skilful use of such grammatical omissions can leave us none the wiser at the end of a long speech or report. Lack of clear language, however, usually means lack of a clear outcome for the communication, to which NLP gives priority. This is not a matter of good grammar, or even efficient use of words, but of effective communication.

Unspecified verbs

Verbs, too, can be missing: 'His attitude bothers me'; 'She blocked the proposal'. 'How did his attitude bother you – what did he *do*?'; 'In what way did she block the proposal – what did she actually *say* or *do*?' Even when a verb *is* used, it may be so general (for instance, travelled, went, learned, helped) that we are still left wondering what was actually done – how, where and when, for instance. This of course is the missing deeper structure of the language. Ask in each case 'How, specifically . . .?' to elicit the meaning which may have been implied but which never got across to your map of understanding.

Nominalisations

Language is replete with catch-all words which avoid specifics. 'I need fulfilment' is a fine sentiment, but is not very helpful in communication terms. What does 'fulfilment' mean, for you, me, or anyone else? What, for instance, needs to *happen* in order that you will be fulfilled? Other *nominalisations* crop up all the time, such as fear, failure, success, impression, management, respect, education, belief, direction, happiness. Each will no doubt have a specific meaning to the communicator, or in some context of the communication, but this is deleted in surface language. We are left guessing, misled and possibly even angry or mistakenly happy. Or we can unravel the meaning to bridge the understanding gap and achieve a mutually better outcome. The acid test is whether you can see, hear and feel the nominalised thing – whether you can wrap it in a parcel. Otherwise it is just a word, without sensory significance or specific meaning other than what the other person cares to give it.

Nominalisations are the black holes of deletions, and you can lose both the significant nouns (who or what) as well as the verbs (what do they actually do?). Like black holes, you can't see them for what they are, as these words are perfectly grammatical; they are also popular with the cream of managers.

You can turn any nominalisation into a verb by asking *who* is doing *what* and *how* exactly are they doing it. Because these patterns can occur in just about every sentence, written or spoken, and in every management and personal context, you will need to be patient in building up the skill both in recognising them and in choosing an effective response. Thankfully, you will have no shortage of opportunity for practice.

Judgements

This language pattern is sometimes termed 'lost performative'. However frightening the linguistic jargon, it concerns a familiar kind of statement – for example, 'Dieting can be dangerous'. Here you need to know the source of the judgement or unwritten standard that is being invoked. 'According to whom?' or 'On what basis, or by what standard?' is the best a judgement deserves, until its source is validated.

Comparisons

The give-away words in this case are comparative terms like 'better' or 'best', ' worse' or 'worst', and any subjective word that requires some comparison to have meaning, such as rich, weak, strong, intelligent and so on. In each case there is a vital missing yardstick of comparison. 'Valerie is a better speaker' demands the question 'Better than whom? And in what way?' Or, 'Intelligent compared with whom – Einstein, your five-year-old daughter, the managers in the southern region – or whom?' The deleted comparisons are often either unrealistic or ludicrous, so there will be little need for debate, but rather a simple identification of the missing part of the meaning. Just ask 'Compared with what, or whom?'

Distortions

Mind reading

Sometimes a statement indicates that one person knows what the other is thinking. 'You're not sure, are you?', or 'I know he didn't enjoy it' are examples, in effect, of mind reading. A deep structure might be 'You are shaking your head, screwing up your eyes, and frowning' in the first case, and 'He had his arms folded all the time, was not looking at the speaker, sat in a slouched position, got up and walked out . . .', and so on.

Another version is when the other person seems to read minds: 'If you cared you would understand how I feel', or 'You should have known I would do that.' Such assumptions may be based on some sort of sensory reading, but the specifics are distorted to form what is rationally an absurd communication. The response is to question how exactly you were expected to know how they felt.

Often a question is answered with another Meta Model pattern. For example: 'He does not appreciate what I do' might be responded to by 'How do you know he does not appreciate you?' The answer, 'Because he never buys me flowers or chocolates', is a complex equivalence. Appreciating someone is equated with buying flowers and chocolates – they purport to have the same meaning, which is at least questionable, if not nonsense. The inclusion of 'never' also adds a universal quantifier to further muddy the waters, and to which a further response 'Never?' could have been made. The aim is to get deeper meaning, better understanding, and a successful transfer of understanding – or communication. In the case of mind reading, ask 'How exactly do you know?' and for reversed mind-reading ask 'How should I know?'

Cause and effect

This is the linking of an assumed cause with an assumed effect. 'The colour makes it cheap' assumes that the cause of its being cheap is the colour. 'I would have finished by now but John wasn't there' again makes a cause and effect statement without the specifics to back it up – the cause of the job not being finished may be that John did not answer his phone at the time the person telephoned, or whatever were the actual circumstances. This is similar to the complex equivalence, although the statements are consequent on one another, sometimes chronologically, rather than applying in parallel. Like several of the Meta Model cases, there are no standard words that will enable you to recognise these every time. The word 'but', however, is sometimes a clue: 'I would have told him *but* he would have gone crazy' – cause: telling him; effect: gone crazy. Note also, in this example, the mind-reading which we often squeeze into our conversation, as well as the emotive nominalisation 'crazy'.

Presuppositions

'I can't begin a new career at my age' is an example of a presupposition. Based on our varied backgrounds and beliefs, presuppositions are an integral part of our filtered view of the world, reflecting personal values and hang-ups. Sometimes 'why' questions have presuppositions built in. 'Why didn't you organise it yourself?', for example, *presupposes* that you did not attempt to do so, that it was your job anyway, that it needed organising, and that the matter is anything to do with the speaker in the first place. This distortion has different formats, of which the salesperson's 'Will you take the red or the black, madam?' is a classic example. This presupposes, of course, that madam is interested in either. But the opportunity for subtlety and distortion is more or less unlimited:

- 'When you think about it, you will understand.' (Presupposition: You have not thought about it, you are dumb, you care in any event, etc.)
- 'Why don't you list them like this?' (You are listing them the wrong way.)
- 'You are as slow as Bob.' (Bob is particularly slow.)
- 'You aren't going to blow it again?' (You have blown it many times before.)

The endless variety will need skill to recognise and counter. Typically, the sort of response: 'What leads you to believe that ...?' will establish the presupposition upon which the communication is based.

The uniqueness of the NLP contribution in this area is to both bring it all together into a coherent model, and offer a series of questions or responses that reverse or clarify the lost and distorted meanings.

Applications for managers

Skilled use of the Meta Model will enable you to:

- quickly get at the heart of an issue, isolating the real problem or issue;
- 'think on your feet'; a knowledge of these patterns and how to respond to them gives extra confidence in group situations, and when fielding questions and criticisms, such as following a presentation.
- detect 'hidden agendas';
- solve problems through progressive questioning of statements; this is a skill we often associate with outstanding leaders who frequently have the ability to expose the critical weakness in an argument or proposal;
- think more clearly;
- take control of your feelings by not overreacting to surface language;
- communicate more effectively by applying Meta Model tests to your own communications; whether one-to-one or groups, or in writing;
- be more assertive, without contrived behaviour;
- positively improve your listening skills;
- get to know how other people think and feel.

You will get the opportunity for practice in all sorts of management situations:

- meetings
- interviews
- discussions with colleagues, your own staff or bosses
- customer or supplier negotiations
- training sessions
- presentations involving questions and comments

- any kind of written communication
- problem-solving

You should apply the Meta Model in stages. Initially, you should not say anything, just learn to recognise the patterns, perhaps confining yourself first to one a day. Note how you feel, having opened up choices of possible meaning, and knowing that, at best, language can only give surface meaning. Then start to form responses mentally, and note again the effect this has on how you feel, but also any insights into the communication you would normally have missed. When you proceed to use the responses verbally, make sure that you do it with a view to maintaining rapport, rather than antagonising. Misuse of the Meta Model is a quick way to break rapport, not to mention relationships. And always keep in mind any outcome you have, even if it is just to know exactly what the other person 'has in mind'.

The Meta Model is an invaluable tool for the communica*tor*, as well as when used by the communica*tee*. You can use it to design your communication in a specific, effective way, with regard to the present understanding and feelings of the other person. You can decide upon an appropriate level of deep structure to suit your specific outcome. You can consciously avoid generalising, omitting, and distorting. Try checking a report you have drafted, or a memo, for Meta Model patterns. See if there is a better form of language that is more likely to fulfil your outcome.

Communication is absolutely central to effective management, as it is to NLP. You now have some principles, models and techniques on which you can form the basis of excellent communication. You cannot not communicate, so it is worth getting it right. But you do have choices. The range of approaches, whether using language, logic, or mental imagery, make use of both the left and right sides of the brain, and any preference you have. Go for what seems useful, and what you will have an opportunity of trying out in everyday work and life. Keep in mind the four-part success cycle – decide what you want, do something, and be flexible enough to change what you do until you get what you want.

◀ PART FOUR ▶

Personal Effectiveness

12

Changing Behaviour

I SAID at the beginning of this book that I was more concerned with you as a *manager* than with *management*, and with practical effectiveness rather than textbook theories. In introducing the theory and practice of NLP I also made it clear that it is more applicable at a personal level than at an organisational level. Having said this, when considering goal achievement and communication, I showed how the principles of NLP can be applied in some cases corporately and to a greater extent to groups. In Part Four I will concentrate again on the manager as an individual.

In offering a science of personal excellence, NLP has a far wider audience than managers, of course. But there is plenty for managers in the different approach of NLP. The theoretical and objective approach is replaced by a cognitive and subjective one. The special role of the manager as communicator and problem-solver also enables him to benefit from those major aspects of the subject. And the manager's privilege of influence over other people means that any increase in *personal* effectiveness is likely to have an organisational impact, besides having repercussions beyond his personal life. NLP sees the manager as a total person, rather than just wearing a work hat. Effectiveness is viewed on a 24-hour basis, and the traditional work/home compartments have to be removed when judging personal excellence and achievement. It is concerned with results and outcomes directly through people, when traditional management has spread its attention more thinly, embracing methods, structures, systems and technology.

Personal effectiveness is captured in the four-part model we met in Chapter 2:

- decide what you want
- take action
- notice what is working and what is not
- change your approach until you achieve what you want.

In this part of the book I will add some more flesh on to this model, including special exercises you can try. But real effectiveness might require a new way of thinking. As a manager you need to become *outcome-oriented*, as we saw in Part Two. This is not so much a question of technique, as a way of life or thinking. And it will probably mean raising your standards, demanding more of yourself both professionally and in your personal life. Consistent success in achieving goals is a continuous upward spiral of effectiveness, and of personal standards and challenge.

Secondly, you will need to change *limiting beliefs*, as well as getting control over feelings. We have already seen how much of our thinking, including beliefs, happens sub-consciously, having an insidious and powerful effect on our behaviour and performance.

Thirdly you need to change your *strategy*. If you have a clear outcome and believe you can achieve it you will find a way – a strategy – that works, even if you have to borrow it from someone else who does well what you want to do, including the values and core beliefs that support their external behaviour.

This suggests the overall aim of *mastery*, a continuous pursuit of personal excellence: mastery over how you feel (your state), over what you do (your behaviour) as well as your relationships and your time. We covered some aspects of time (including timelines) and of relationships in Part Three. In this part of the book I want to concentrate mainly on mastery and successful strategies, both for thinking (feelings, beliefs, attitudes) and behaviour.

EFFECTIVE BEHAVIOUR

Effectiveness depends on what you do. Information is power – but it's not what you know, its *what you do with what you know* that makes the difference. Results, or outputs, are achieved by actions rather than lofty thoughts or dreams. This can work two ways, of course, and negative behaviour – especially the habitual variety – can be responsible for much of a manager's ineffectiveness. Activist, hands-on managers, so prized by top management, may be carrying out the wrong actions and going in the wrong direction.

The importance of *goal-related* action was made clear in the four-stage success model, and also in the cybernetic model of goal achievement. NLP emphasises not just the need for outcomes, but the importance of behaviour being congruent with those outcomes. A moment's reflection will reveal the common sense of this. The effectiveness of a manager is not measured by the scale or complexity of activity, but by whether he achieves his and the organisation's goals.

Acting without thinking

NLP also recognises that most of our behaviour is carried out unconsciously, in the simple sense that we don't have to think about what we are doing. This applies to all sorts of habitual activities, from getting dressed and washed, to driving a car or balancing a ledger. So the unconscious part of our thinking – the submerged part of the mental iceberg – has its counterpart also in that part of our *behaviour* which, at the time, does not involve conscious thought. Some experts talk about well over 90 per cent of our thinking being of this sort, and you may find it interesting to list your everyday behaviours and see what proportion of your time is spent in automatic or semi-automatic behaviour. Most managers I meet in seminars are familiar with driving long distances without thinking about the actual driving (i.e. what they are doing), and in sport 'thinking' tends to be about strategy or tactics, rather than actual behaviour. Even technical work can become routine, so that we are not conscious of our behaviour. As well as being concerned with higher aspects of the work, the mind will wander on to anything else it cares to, whether this is another problem at work, or domestic and social matters. Meanwhile habitual behaviour carries on, usually with remarkable effectiveness.

Towards unconscious competence

This automatic pilot facility we all have is one of the bases of individual achievement and excellence. NLP uses the term *unconscious competence*, which forms part of a powerful model for learning effectiveness. There are four stages.

- *Unconscious incompetence* (or unconscious ignorance). This is the state in which we are not aware of a certain short-coming in our accumulated knowledge or skill. A wander around the reference section of a library will usually reveal whole subjects which you were not aware of. Until we have emerged from this stage, which is something easily observed in children as they continuously discover new aspects of their world, there will be no learning and personal effectiveness.
- *Conscious incompetence* (or conscious ignorance). This is an important stage in our learning, opening up the possibility of new knowledge, understanding and skills. Most adults confess to massive areas of knowledge, perhaps to do with their work, hobbies and interests, in which they are sadly and very consciously lacking. It is this realisation that motivates us to acquire new knowledge and try new skills.
- *Conscious competence.* By learning and training we can reach a level of competence. Most people, if they are honest, will have one or two things they are 'good at', at least to a certain level.
- *Unconscious competence.* This is the really important stage in terms of excellence. There are numerous activities we carry out without thinking, hardly appreciating their complexity in terms of the physiological feats involved. I have already mentioned actions we take for granted, like getting dressed and driving a car. The competence involved is apparent when others who have not achieved that level wonder how you can do such things without thinking. A non-swimmer or non-driver, or a child struggling to learn to tie shoelaces, however, knows well the competence involved in activities others take for granted. Similar comparisons are made with people who are adept at mental arithmetic, drawing, or playing music 'by ear'. Such people usually do not know what the fuss is about, because their competence

is largely unconscious. They don't think about it – if they did, they would probably mess up the activity – and certainly have difficulty explaining in detail how they do it.

The conscious mind can only handle a few thoughts at one time, so clearly will not do well if it has to think about all the activities involved in, say, driving a car. In a learning mode we are very conscious of not being able to remember everything at once, whether operating a machine at work, driving a car, or playing the piano. Only with repetition do we become competent, and with further practice carry out the whole complex activity without thinking – unconsciously. Think back to when you first tried something you are now skilled at. Excellence usually looks easy, whether it is the squash player occupying the middle of the court as his opponent chases around him, or the tennis champion who seems to play with childlike abandon even when everything depends on a single shot, or the mother who can handle so many things at once. And that's the way it should be, when we reach the state of unconscious competence.

The easy way to effectiveness

There are three important aspects to this concept of unconscious competence as far as your personal effectiveness is concerned.

Doing several things at once

First, when the basic activity you are carrying out does not occupy your conscious mind, you are able to use your mind on other things. That is an invaluable management trick. When playing tennis, rather than thinking about the stroke, you can think about important tactical and strategic matters, and so gain a competitive edge. If you can take a major conference speech in your stride, you can pay attention to special aspects of it, being more aware of the reaction of the audience, picking up on the themes of other speakers, and so on. That special freedom to focus on what is important, rather than the mechanics of behaviour, is what turns competence into excellence or mastery.

The principle applies in any area of business or personal life.

If the salesperson's basic presentation technique is unconscious, he can concentrate more fully on the specific circumstances of the situation and customer, and particular
outcomes. A manager who has unconscious competence in the
various management skills can think about the unique aspects
of a situation, focusing on outcomes rather than the many
processes involved. This, it seems, is a characteristic of leaders
as compared with managers.

A 'freed-up' mind will be more open to intuition and
insights, adding quality and originality to thinking. It is also a
feature of good communicators. They seem so *natural*, not
needing to think about the mechanics of the communication,
which otherwise produces a contrived, incongruent behaviour
that is usually detected. We might say of such a person, 'She
gets along easily with anyone', or 'He makes you feel
completely at ease.' That is communication at the level of
unconscious competence.

Optimal performance

Secondly, as well as being able to do several things at once, and
particularly being able to concentrate on what you decide is
important, you actually perform *better*. As well as exercising
physical skills, you will be a better tactician, strategist, overall
manager or leader. Conversely, however proficient we are at a
skill, conscious interference will tend to reduce our competence. Try concentrating on the different aspects of your
driving, the mechanics of fastening your tie, playing a musical
instrument, or typing. At best, your behaviour lacks flow and
any sort of grace. More likely, you will become a self-conscious
incompetent. The human cybernetic system works best
automatically.

Modelling others

Thirdly, NLP allows us to model excellence in others. That is,
although we may not be conscious of what we are doing that
produces certain behaviour and results, it is possible to elicit
mental and behavioural strategies, and in effect copy them.
And it is these strategies, or programs of unconscious competence, that provide the basis for excellence. Modelling is
covered further in the next chapter.

New Behaviour Generator

NLP has different ways to change behaviour. A popular one I describe below, known as the New Behaviour Generator, is for changing any of your own behaviour that you are not satisfied with, or generating new behaviour. It is based on the three main sensory representation systems you have already met when visualising communication outcomes – seeing, hearing, and feeling. Its power lies in the fact that the unconscious brain can hardly distinguish between a real behaviour and one which is vividly imagined. So, for instance, if your mind was elsewhere during a boring lecture, your reality for that period was what you imagined, or daydreamed, rather than the lecture room of which you were temporarily unconscious. The same would apply when you make a car journey and do not remember the external sights and places – but you nevertheless experienced the reality of your thoughts. Sometimes thoughts can be so vivid, such as in dreaming, that on reflection you are not sure when something is real or imagined. The disorientation that is experienced on waking from a vivid dream starkly illustrates that our experience of reality happens in the mind – it is created in your brain.

This is an invaluable principle, and is the basis for using various visualisation techniques in which forthcoming situations can be experienced in advance. As we saw in Part Two, it is an effective 'right brain' boost to goal-setting. As a manager you can use the New Behaviour Generator to give you confidence where you are lacking it, which could be giving an important presentation to the main board, speaking at a professional conference, conducting a disciplinary interview, or chairing a meeting. Or you can use it as a motivator, say to keep your desk tidy or to get on with important work that doesn't appeal to you. Outside work, it can be applied to any habitual behaviour you are keen to change, or a new behaviour, such as a sport or pastime that you are a bit unsure about.

1. First identify the behaviour you want to change, or the new behaviour you want to acquire.
2. Describe the new behaviour, asking yourself how you would look, sound and feel if you were doing the new behaviour.
3. Now see yourself doing the behaviour as you want to in the

context you will use it. Note all the sights, sounds and feelings, and be aware of the response of other people involved in your movie. If you cannot see yourself doing it, imagine someone else who you know or imagine could do it.

4. If there is anything about what you see that you are unhappy about, go back and perfect it in your mind. Make changes that satisfy you.

5. When you are satisfied with your performance, step inside the picture and become yourself, running through the behaviour as though you are actually doing it now. Again, be aware of all the sights, sounds and feelings, and the response of others involved.

6. You can still change anything you wish, by going back to stage 3. Check how any changes you make feel when you have stepped back into the picture yourself.

7. When you are happy with your new behaviour, think of a signal you will see, hear or feel, internally or externally, that will let you know it is time to use your new behaviour. For example, the signal might be going into a certain room, seeing a certain person's face, stepping on to a podium, getting a sinking feeling in your stomach, or whatever.

8. Now run it right through. Imagine the signal happening, carrying out your new behaviour, and being aware of the feeling of satisfaction and achievement.

Many consistent achievers are found to use some variation of this process, which is one of the keys to personal effectiveness.

Creating experience

You can now arrange your diary and circumstances so that you get the opportunity to carry out your new behaviour. The model can be used in all sorts of situations, and the more you use it the more effective it will become. Whenever you are confronted with situations in which you want to change your behaviour, you can run through the New Behaviour Generator and immediately feel more confident. This new confidence is based on *real experience* as far as your brain is concerned. The more mental practice you get, the more confident you will be as you build up a track record of 'hard disc' brain experience. And the more confident you are the more you will do justice to your own abilities and skills when you come to change actual behaviour. So remind yourself of the important rules of clear, vivid representation, and repetition.

Getting mentally fit

If you have difficulty making this work you may need to allow yourself more practice in creating realistic internal representations. Anything is possible, but, as with an atrophied limb, you may need to have some exercise before you are proficient and mentally fit. Another possibility is that what you want to do is not well-formed or ecologically sound. Go back to the criteria for a well-formed outcome in Part Two, and particularly to the importance of ecology. If there are other internal forces that cause your unwanted behaviour, you will have to sort out these outcomes and decide what your priorities are, and how one outcome may affect others. Often this will become apparent when you 'future pace' your new behaviour and register how you feel about it. Unconscious intentions will usually reveal themselves, at least as uncomfortable feelings, when you experience the new behaviour.

Having established the importance of behaviour in achieving outcomes, and how you can make actual changes, you need to be aware that outward behaviour is only part of the story. Effectiveness is also to do with how we feel, and our attitudes and beliefs, which I address in the next chapter.

13

Harnessing Feelings and Beliefs

HOW you *feel* will invariably affect how you behave. Personal mastery includes emotional mastery. Just about everything we do has its effect on how we feel – usually our intention is to feel happy at achieving whatever goal we are after. That is the essence of the outcome model of changing from one state to another we met in Part One. Mind and body are tied up together in the goal package.

Feelings affect behaviour, and this works in both a positive and a negative way. If you feel under the weather, or lack motivation, your behaviour will reflect this, and you might well go for hours without producing any worthwhile outputs. Conversely, when you feel good and on form, you seem able to produce miracles – and indeed your behaviour can be many times more effective than at other times. These feelings, of course, are no more under our conscious control than habitual behaviour. If we could rationalise them away, they would not be such a problem. Similarly, if we could turn on an empowering feeling at will, our lives would surely be transformed. Fortunately NLP enables us to understand and control feelings; rather than trying to suppress them or put them down to chance or serendipity, we can use them to achieve our outcomes. As well as generating new behaviour, we need to generate new, more empowering, or appropriate feelings.

Emotional triggers

Let's establish just how volatile and sensitive our feelings are. The most innocuous word, gesture, facial expression or sensation can change how you feel – the sound of a telephone ringing, a smell bringing back memories, or even a colour. For example, the thud of a buff envelope on the doormat, or a strange sound from under the car bonnet, can create an instant sinking feeling, while the voice of someone you care for can instantly transform your day for the better. We can rationalise these things, of course, but it isn't very effective – feelings seem to have a life of their own. Emotional triggers, whether a help or a hindrance, may be the critical factor in your outcome.

In communication, for instance, how each party feels about the other, or the subject being communicated, will often be many times more powerful a factor in producing an outcome – or not producing an outcome, as the case may be – than all the outward, rational aspects of the message and its delivery. So there is lots of mileage in being able to control how you feel, especially those feelings which recur and affect your behaviour and achievements habitually.

EXERCISE

How to feel good in sixty seconds

The more confident you become at accessing and using your subjective experience – your inner senses – the more you will be able to use your knowledge and skill to take control over feelings as well as behaviour. Try this exercise.

- Make a score of 1 to 10 to reflect how you feel right now. A top score of ten means you are on top of the world, and a low score reflects the converse.

- Think back to a most pleasurable experience, perhaps when you achieved something really worthwhile, got special recognition, and for whatever reason were, at the time, on cloud nine. Re-experience the occasion, dwelling first on the sights, then sounds, then all the associated feelings of the memory. Bring all your inner experiences together and savour for a while the experience, just as though you were living it all over again.

- Come gently back to the present and score how you now feel.

The chances are that your score – how you now feel – will have been affected by your recollection of the earlier experience. So by thinking, you can change how you feel. If you are in any doubts (you may have been feeling euphoric when you did the first score) do it the other way round – this time think of an unpleasant, embarrassing or distasteful memory, and again note the effect. The message is simple: you can have control over your feelings if you want to and know how to.

Feelings and physiology

There is another important feature of feelings, which provides a further opportunity for control. Feelings are very much linked to our bodies. When you are carrying out a cerebral, left-brain calculation or logical deduction you may be poker-faced, not betraying what you are thinking. But feelings are far more likely to be revealed in the many characteristics of your physiology, from pulse and breathing rate, tone and pitch of voice, to all the nuances of body language. So at this basic level there is a relationship between feelings and behaviour, and the relationship is two-way. How you feel affects your body, and what you do with your body affects how you feel. Try taking on all the characteristics of an unhappy person, including posture and facial expression. Keep it up for a while and you start to become unhappy. Or try acting exactly as you would if you were very happy and just note the change in how you feel. So feelings can be changed by thinking differently (in your control), or behaving differently (also in your control), or both. Your behaviour in achieving outcomes is now supported by positive, motivating feelings, and your feelings are supported by the way you act.

TRANSFORMING ATTITUDES AND BELIEFS

Habitual feelings develop into attitudes that can be entrenched, affecting our behaviour more or less permanently. A major change of strategy, such as becoming optimistic, or having a more positive attitude, can change your behaviour and performance dramatically.

Attitudes, like feelings, concern how we interpret things. A tiny cloud in the distance will be interpreted differently depending on whether you are optimistic or pessimistic. Our interpretations of personal behaviour are described in NLP as 'excuses'. Everything we do is supported by an excuse. We have to have a reason or purpose for whatever we do, whether our actions seem good or bad to us. And our excuses may relate to how we feel, what we believe, our attitudes, or how we see ourselves – our self-image. Spilling the coffee might therefore be explained by the fact that you are overworked, distracted, clumsy, careless, or stupid. Or maybe you were concentrating, engrossed in your work, a free spirit, or whatever. Each behaviour is interpreted, and that interpretation, or excuse, will align (whether consciously or unconsciously) with our beliefs, values or self-image. So most behaviour is habitual, because our beliefs and values are habitual – we tend to stick with them without giving them conscious thought. So beliefs and habitual behaviour are mutually self-fulfilling – they feed on each other. You tend to do whatever fits what you believe about yourself, and your beliefs tend to reflect what you know you do.

Excuses

These interpretations, or excuses, determine the quality of our lives. In effect we are ruled by our 'inner interpreter'. Before describing a pattern you can use to transform your inner interpreter, there are some important principles involved. These excuses can be put into three categories: time, place and person. This simple model, and the effect of our excuses on behaviour, is based on the extensive work of Martin Seligman. Notice first the *difference* in these categories, then when you do the exercise you can choose the interpretation you apply to specific behaviours.

Time

An excuse can be permanent or temporary. 'It's all over', or 'You will never finish that' are examples of statements that interpret in a final, permanent way. However, 'This has not worked out the way we intended' or 'That chance has passed' are more temporary. There is room for a change in the future, and the behaviour in question does not become entrenched.

Place

Excuses can be either pervasive or specific. Examples of pervasive statements are: 'I can't sell', 'teachers are arrogant' or 'I'm a failure'. Remember the universal quantifiers you met in the Meta Model in Chapter 11. *Specific* statements are: 'I didn't manage to sell to so-and-so, on that occasion', 'Geoff (a teacher) is arrogant' or 'I failed that time'. 'I failed' is a matter of fact our brains can cope with. 'I am a failure' is pervasive and does not leave room for hope; neurologically, it is an ideal self-fulfilling instruction.

Person

Excuses can be personal or impersonal. 'I'm untidy', 'I'm irresponsible' and 'I'm to blame' are examples of personal interpretations. The impersonal equivalents might be: 'That job I did was untidy', 'I acted irresponsibly' or ' I'm to blame for so-and-so'. You literally become more objective about the behaviour in question, which is defined more specifically, and you can choose whether and how you will change your behaviour in the future.

Temporary, specific, and impersonal excuses have far less effect on our behaviour than permanent, pervasive and personal excuses. As we saw in the Meta Model, our surface language interpretations may be irrational or unlikely in any event, and so can usually be switched into a less permanent, personal or pervasive form, without kidding ourselves. In this way, not only do we feel better about behaviour we do not like, but by changing the dimension of our excuse we can break self-fulfilling behaviour patterns that only thrive because of the excuses we give them.

_____ EXERCISE _____

Your inner interpreter

This is an effective way to approach changing your attitude about behaviour. The following is a pattern that gets your inner interpreter working for you rather than against you. For this exercise, be ready to use your imagination in a simple, childlike way. Remember you are dealing with subconscious parts of your thinking, so addressing the logical, rational side of the brain – with the most plausible criticism – is unlikely to have any effect. We need to get in touch with parts of us that usually go unknown and unhindered.

1. Think of a specific time when something didn't turn out the way you wanted.

2. Ask yourself how you explain the way it happened. Listen carefully to your inner interpreter as an interpretation emerges, and write down what you hear. If you can, note where (which direction, in space or inside you) the 'voice' is coming from.

3. Repeat the first two steps using two more events which have emotional importance to you.

4. Now look at the three interpretations you've written down, noting them for permanence, pervasiveness, and personality. Check what is similar between them.

5. Rewrite the explanations so that they are more optimistic, making them specific to a time or occasion, and to the place they happened. Then make them impersonal, in effect separating you from your behaviour.

6. Try to detect where in space these different explanations came from. You may have to go back and experience them again. Did they all come from the same direction?

7. Realise that this inner interpreter is a vital part of you that helps to explain the world, and start to appreciate its concern for your welfare. Thank it for bringing you to where you are today.

8. Now you are in communication, use your inner interpreter to come up with even more positive excuses for your three experiences or behaviours. New interpretations may well come to your mind.

9. Imagine the voice moves to your elbow, and it becomes like a familiar TV newscaster! Try moving the source of the voice down to your little finger, and change the tone of voice again – make it friendly and familiar – maybe like a ten-year-old child, or a cartoon character. Then listen as your interpreter voices the new excuses you thought of and other optimistic ones. Check how you now feel about your three emotionally important experiences with these new explanations. Savour your enjoyment for a while.

10. Let your interpreter go back to where it started, or where it feels best, but give it the voice you find most reassuring, compelling and motivating.

Let your interpretations come to you instinctively – there is no forcing involved. Some might arise easily from conscious analysis, or plain common sense. Others might just occur to you. Or if you get stuck, why not imagine what your interpretation of an event or behaviour would be *if there was one!* The unconscious mind responds sometimes amazingly to the silliest games and 'pretend' devices. But if you do want examples, here are ways you might have interpreted, say losing a big contract to a rival firm, after you have given the final presentation to the client:

● 'We always seem to fall down on price [quality/response time/after sales service/etc.].'
● 'That's the worst I've done.'
● 'It's all we could have hoped for in the circumstances.'
● 'I went on too long.'
● 'That's the last chance we'll get with them.'
● 'Well, you win some, you lose some!'
● 'I knew it was slipping away from us.'

- 'There's something been going on behind the scenes.'
- 'Ours was the best proposal in the end.'
- 'I'm no good at these formal selling do's.'
- 'It was a fluke; we should have sewn it up.'
- 'It was just like me to throw it away after all the effort.'

These responses reflect different possible personal scenarios, but in practice even a single event might produce a number of different excuses. You might like to try to amend these, and your own excuses using the time/place/personal model. What you are after is to transform your *attitude* which will in turn change your *future behaviour* and thus increase your chances of success.

'That's the worst I've done' could take you deeper into a personal negative, hopeless self-belief that could easily produce an even greater horror at the next proposal. Whereas, 'That was a fluke; we should have had it sewn up' might spur you to set the record right in an impressive way at the earliest opportunity. Each excuse will affect your future behaviour. And behaviour is what produces hard outcomes.

The bottom line is that you are free to interpret what you do, or what happens, in any way you like. Few of the interpretations we make (just like the examples above) are based on fact in any event – they are more likely to be judgements, feelings, or beliefs. And all these are subjective and changeable – at no cost, and with obvious potential benefits. Get your inner interpreter on your side. He has you at heart, and his excuses are meant to help.

This is another technique for directly changing behaviour, as well as how you feel. It works well with habitual behaviour ('Why on earth do I keep doing that?') that you know stops your achievement and pleasure, but which you seem somehow locked into, however hard you try consciously. A new interpretation is likely to suggest other behaviours which will bring about what you wanted more successfully. So you don't lose out by giving up a familiar, long-standing behaviour – you achieve your outcome, but in a way you, as a total person, are happier with. By putting a more positive, optimistic interpretation on everything you do you will become more goal-directed and you will achieve more. And because you will be getting to know yourself better, you will also enjoy a stronger self-image and sense of personal identity.

EMPOWERING AND DISEMPOWERING BELIEFS

As we have just seen, a positive attitude will do wonders for performance, while a pessimistic attitude can be uncannily self-fulfilling. Beliefs operate like unquestioned commands given to automatons. They shape every action and feeling, and determine whether we will achieve or miss our goals. How you *perceive* something makes all the difference, and you are free to see things from any perspective you wish. Beliefs and values are even more long-standing than feelings and attitudes, which change over time. When you believe something, you act as if it were true. And acting in such a way – believing you are able, that a goal is within your power, that you deserve it – almost guarantees you will achieve what you are after.

Misinterpreting experience

Beliefs often go back to childhood, and can be influenced by authority figures, repetitive experiences, and sometimes traumas. They are usually generalisations about our past, based on our interpretation of pleasurable and painful experiences, and are our best strategy for surviving and succeeding. As it happens, we don't consciously decide what we are going to believe, whatever the rationale or implications of our beliefs. In fact, many of our beliefs can be based on *misinterpretations* of past experience. We forget that beliefs are no more than perceptions, usually with a limited sell-by date, yet we act as though they were concrete realities. They give meaning to everything we do. So real and lasting change has got to include changing beliefs.

It's not events that shape us, but what we believe those events mean. Survivors of the Nazi holocaust seemed to grasp on to a belief that they would come through to tell others what they had endured. Research with people suffering from

multiple personality disorder has shown complete physiological change as the patients moved from one personality
belief to another – in some cases, symptoms of diabetes or high
blood pressure switching with each change. So whatever their
origin or rationale, and even when operating outside our
consciousness, beliefs are very real in terms of behaviour and
performance – and even our survival.

Believing in your outcome

Before embarking on the greatest strategy, you need to believe
that you can and will succeed. Belief that you are able and
deserving of an outcome has been shown to be a bigger factor
in eventual success than technical skills or positive outside
circumstances. Belief that there is a solution to your problem
provides the important motivation to solve it, and triggers the
unconscious associations needed.

You are what you believe. Our beliefs shape us, motivate us,
and act as guiding principles, giving stability and continuity.
Many beliefs about the world around and its laws are held in
common, and this creates rapport and a sense of community.
Other beliefs apply to our company, groups of people like
clients or bosses, or individual people. And every such belief
affects how we behave.

Believing in yourself

When it comes to personal effectiveness, beliefs about yourself
play the biggest part. These make up your self-image and have
a major, direct effect on every part of your behaviour. A single
belief about yourself, such as 'I am good at organising things'
or 'I easily lose concentration' can have an effect on whole
areas of behaviour and outcomes. Unlike a feeling, which may
be gone half-way through the morning after you have put your
mind to something else, or even a few minutes after meeting
someone who has had a positive impact on you, beliefs are
more permanent and insidious. Usually we *know* when we *feel*
particularly good or bad, but we are largely unaware of the
effect that long-held beliefs have on our behaviour – they
become part of our automatic system, whether empowering or
disempowering. All-embracing beliefs such as 'Life is . . .',

'People are . . .', 'I am . . .' can have a completely overriding impact on all our behaviour.

Amazingly, all this potential 'belief power' for human excellence usually goes untapped, and indeed unrecognised. Using the familiar iceberg analogy, behaviour is what is visible, feelings and attitudes operate a bit below the surface, and beliefs and values at a deeper level still. The deeper the belief, and the more unconscious we are of it, the more leverage it will have on our behaviour.

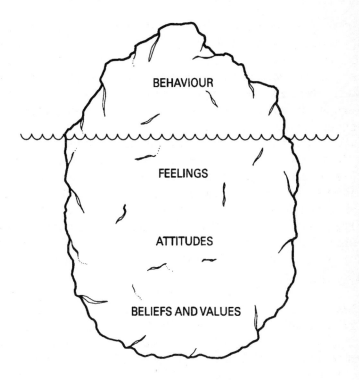

FIGURE 8 Below the surface factors in behaviour

Although beliefs do not figure in the usual factors for super management, modern managers who operate ignoring the submerged part of the behavioural iceberg are severely limiting themselves. Even in hard-nosed problem-solving, it has been shown that if you *believe* there is a solution to a problem you stand a much better chance of finding one. Unless you *believe* it is possible to reach a goal, you are unlikely to achieve it. And

self-beliefs, such as 'I'm no good at speaking in front of a
crowd' are consistently and powerfully self-fulfilling. In short,
beliefs are so powerful that they can be masters that govern our
every behaviour and achievement. The good news is that –
being no more or less than mental programs or strategies –
they can be changed and used to bring about our conscious
intentions.

Believe what you want to

You can believe what you want to – the choice is yours. And as
it happens, we do change our beliefs over a period. Think
about things that you believe today which once you did not,
and things you don't believe today which you once believed.
Such change, however, is the exception rather than the rule,
and usually something major is required to rock us out of our
familiar mindsets. If you don't think you are artistic, you may
need lots of successes and convincing from friends to believe
what may have been true all along – that in fact you have
artistic talents. The problem is that beliefs are self-fulfilling,
and we are so ingenious at justifying our behaviour in line with
our beliefs that our actual behaviour is affected. Eventually we
prove to others as well as ourselves that we are right. But self-
fulfilling belief can be made to work in our favour, and
positive, empowering beliefs can be left alone to form spirals of
seemingly effortless competence and achievement.

All this is more to do with our individual perceptive maps
than with any logic or reality. And the software of thinking,
including beliefs and other strategies for behaviour, may just
need a new program. All these aspects of thinking act as filters
on our behaviour before ever we achieve the outcomes we
desire.

Rules that support beliefs

The behavioural rules we follow are simply the common-sense
(to us) outworking of our beliefs. If you believe staff respond to
strong leadership rather than consensus-type management,
you will act accordingly:

- don't give away too much information to subordinates;

- don't appear to be weak;
- be decisive, even when you may not have all the facts – that's a manager's job;
- don't get too pally with junior staff;
- measure by performance only;
- learn not to trust anyone;

and so on.

Specific supporting rules

If you believe you are better at one-to-one communication than speaking in public, your rules might include:

- avoid up-front presentations;
- stick to informal rather than formal meetings;
- get to know people personally and persuade them of your views one by one;
- leave public events early if you may be called upon to give an impromptu speech;
- work out excuses not to attend where you know your role will involve up-front communication;
- find an immediate subordinate who can quickly fill in for you if you go sick or have to collect your child from school;
- arrange to have a couple of drinks beforehand whenever you have to speak publicly;
- don't run departmental meetings but communicate by memos or through section heads;
- delegate client work that will involve prepared presentations;
- go clammy, breathe quickly and sweat whenever you get on your feet in front of a group.

Supporting reference props

In the case of personal beliefs, such as 'I am likeable', we also have supporting references for our beliefs. These might include 'I can easily start a conversation with strangers', 'I have a large circle of friends', 'I have a steady marriage', 'I have had a successful career', etc. The more references we have, and the more these are backed by sensory experience (we can easily imagine doing something, whatever the real track record) the stronger will be the belief they support. Other experience will support other beliefs, such as 'I am disorganised' or 'I am assertive'. A lot of reference props might therefore have to be knocked away (whether real or imagined) before a belief is changed. Conversely, a belief can be created by marshalling a few supporting experiences, or representations of experience.

These references, behavioural rules or strategies go unnoticed, and you don't get to write them down, as you might corporate or personal objectives. But they affect your behaviour and of course your outcomes. Changing beliefs means that you will have to change a number of operating rules, or mental networks, or you would not be acting congruently. So to ensure that what you do is directed towards what you want, you need to:

- identify your beliefs;
- recognise whether they are empowering or disempowering in relation to your current outcomes (rather than historical outcomes and values);
- identify the rules they spawn, so that you know the effect;
- identify the references they draw upon, to check their present validity;
- replace your beliefs with more appropriate, empowering ones.

Identifying beliefs

Let's start with identifying beliefs. We have seen that the rules that confirm our beliefs result in actions – they affect how we work and live. Jot down a list of your typical actions throughout the day and see if you can match them with some corresponding belief or value. On a cold winter's morning the act of getting out of bed in the first place might hinge on a belief in the work ethic, giving a fair day's work for a fair day's pay, in doing the best to provide for your family, or being a lackey to your firm or a stick in the mud; or values to do with conscientiousness, loyalty, professionalism, punctuality, setting an example, or whatever. You may find this personally revealing.

Having identified beliefs to go with your list of actions, you will probably be able to add to the list by thinking about the issues they raise. Otherwise, carry on listing actions in various situations and other beliefs will be identified. After a while you will keep returning to the same list of beliefs – there is a finite number, although the supporting rules will probably be extensive.

Some common examples of negative or disempowering beliefs

- I feel awkward in a large social gathering
- I can't draw a straight line
- I'm tone deaf
- I couldn't make a speech if you paid me
- I'm a bit of a loner
- I just can't remember names
- My mind easily goes blank
- I can't concentrate for long
- I could never be a boss
- I have a terrible accent
- I am hopeless with anything academic
- I'm a slow reader
- I'm not mechanically minded
- I'm stubborn like my father
- I'm never on time

Choosing empowering beliefs

The next step is to decide whether you are happy with your own beliefs – the above are just examples – bearing in mind that some of them will have been operating unconsciously, and most of them will have origins that go back a long time. When you think in terms of outcomes, or purpose, the big question is whether these beliefs are helping you or hindering you in the achievement of your outcomes. In NLP terms, are they empowering or disempowering? This will depend on your outcomes – an apparently negative belief, such as 'I can't draw a straight line' may not affect you in your present job and circumstances, unless you need to draw straight lines. On the other hand, a belief like 'I'm hopeless at mental arithmetic' would be disempowering if your work requires numeracy. Having said this, in the first example the belief might have prevented you from pursuing a hobby or interest, or even a career opportunity that you may have wished for. Perhaps you once fancied working in a field involving graphics or design, but dismissed it out of hand – this is the effect a negative belief, whether rational or irrational, tends to have. Or you may want to try a new hobby that involves drawing skills, that might involve a lot of pleasure and a new world of interest, but again the negative belief will usually stop you from even making the first enquiries. So any such belief can be disempowering in terms of your wider life and in the longer term, even though it does not impact on today's goals. Quite simply, it represents a limitation on what you can achieve.

In the numeracy example, which may affect you more directly as a manager, there are usually further indirect negative results of such disempowering beliefs. For example, a few beliefs of this sort can support, in your hierarchy of beliefs, a more ubiquitous belief about your level of intelligence, how bright you are, or whether you are a slow learner. So there is a lot of mileage to be got in identifying and replacing any beliefs that are disempowering. Your personal map of what is possible will be enlarged and enriched, and you will have more choices.

───────────── EXERCISE ─────────────

How to change disempowering beliefs

So how can we change beliefs which we have identified as not supporting our outcomes? As with changing behaviours, there are different approaches. Here is a popular example, usually called the belief change pattern. You have already seen how important it is to harness your natural, internal representation systems in bringing about change. In the following, and other NLP patterns, you may have to suspend belief for a little while, and certainly put to one side any logical, professional scepticism that interferes with the simple but effective right-brain activities.

1. First identify a belief that is disempowering, and that you would like to change.

2. Next, identify what you would rather believe, stating it in

a positive form. Make sure it is your belief, rather than someone else's, and something you are able to change if you wish. Also make sure it is about a *process*, rather than static perfection (for example, it is better to believe you are getting *better* at public speaking than that you are an expert public speaker). Check also on the ecology, as you did with outcomes in Chapter 5.

3. Create labels – A4 sheets of paper will do – identifying each of six locations of change: current belief; open to doubt; museum of old beliefs; preferred belief; open to belief; and sacred or special place.

4. Place these labels on the floor in a clockwise direction, as though they are place settings around an imaginary dinner table.

5. Step from one location to the next, thinking of a vivid experience which fits each description. For example, a time when you were open to doubt about an issue or a person, or a belief that once you held but is now just a museum belief that no longer affects your life; a time when you were open to believing something (perhaps as you became more aware of the facts, or were persuaded by a respected friend); and times that illustrate beliefs that are about as important as life itself - the sacred place. This establishes 'location anchors' for each belief state.

6. Standing in the 'current belief' location, experience again your limiting belief.

7. Taking it with you, move on to 'open to doubt', and notice how you now doubt your limiting belief.

8. Now step into the 'museum of old beliefs', again experiencing your limiting belief as a discarded one in the museum.

9. Leave it in the 'museum of old beliefs', and now step into your 'preferred belief' location and experience it fully.

10. Now move into the 'open to belief' location and feel yourself open to believing your new belief is true.

11. Take your preferred belief and step into the 'sacred place',

noting how special and indispensable your preferred belief now is to you.

12. Finally, taking with you your sacred place feelings about your preferred belief, step back into your 'current belief' location, noting how you now feel about it.

If you need to, change the place names, or change the way you symbolise the important belief stages – just make sure each belief stage is represented. But bear in mind that how we feel is linked to our behaviour, and sometimes a change of state can happen easily by the simplest change of position or physiology. In other words, these NLP strategies usually have a lot of method to their apparent madness.

This exercise can be applied to any belief. The more proficient you become at experiencing each stage, using actual experiences from memory, of course, the more strongly you will be able to imprint changes. You will probably want to start with those self-beliefs you have already identified as disempowering. There will be many outcomes you find you can achieve, once you have created more empowering beliefs to support them.

◄ 14 ►

Modelling Strategies for Success

THE early NLP work was concerned with modelling excellence in particular outstanding individuals, and the idea of modelling is still central. NLP is the study of excellence, and modelling is the process used to specifically identify and 'code' excellence so that others can also achieve it. Modern life accustoms us to admiring feats of human achievement as having almost mystical qualities, and special skills and abilities are often explained away in terms of genetics, serendipity, or positive thinking. Some put it all down to practice, or perseverance. Sadly, the world is replete with disciplined, determined people who seem to put a lot more effort into their mediocrity than excellent people seem to expend on their success. Indeed, one of the recurring features of personal excellence is that it seems so easy and natural. Skill and what may be called genius, rather than gruelling effort, is what distinguishes those at the top of the pile.

Strategies that work

Purposeful behaviour is linked to specific mental strategies, which are essentially brain software – dynamic and programmable rather than fixed systems such as those that control our breathing and pulse, for instance. Synaptic connections in the brain, of which there are many billions, and infinitely more potentially, happen when we use the brain, whether to think or control our behaviour. These 'strategies' are formed naturally as part of the modelling tendency. You only need to watch a child growing up in a home where the father is a football enthusiast to see the natural tendency of the child to model behaviour. A similar effect is seen if the child is surrounded by artists, cooks, readers, swimmers, cyclists or whatever. Television also has an enormous influence, and negative or antisocial behaviour is just as likely to be modelled as positive behaviour. So the modelling process is as instinctive as the cybernetic goal-achieving tendency we have already met, and just as powerful a factor when it comes to acquiring skills. NLP simply makes it possible to model in a positive, conscious way, so the uncertainty and mystique are taken out of the process.

The mental dimension

Positive thinking, of course, recognises the importance of the mental dimension. And there is no doubt that a positive, optimistic attitude will achieve more than a negative, pessimistic one. But, other than motivators like writing your goals down, or self talk, which only seem to work for people who are already positively inclined (that is, they have a strategy in place) and which usually have just short-term results, a broad philosophical approach to excellence will not work. Moreover, it can be very frustrating and sometimes counter-productive if you identify a weakness and try hard consciously to overcome it, but achieve no lasting results.

From our understanding of how the brain works it is now clear that most of its operation is unconscious, so we need to tap into that massive, subterranean part of our thinking. But managers, like other professionals, like to stick to logical, left-brain processes, and are usually reluctant to adapt to new knowledge and skills in the natural way that a child does. Consequently, many people do not advance in many areas, right through their adult life, and for instance, might have no more personal skill at drawing and music than when they were ten years old. That is not the fault of the brain, however, and amazingly some older people learn a number of new skills and develop major new interests, when the constraints of working institutions and social expectations are behind them. NLP gives us the choice to decide on what we want to achieve, and to borrow strategies of excellence from wherever we find them. For practical purposes, there are no limits to what we can achieve with our standard, god-like neurophysiological goal-achieving system.

Differences

Modelling takes a similar approach to the four-part success pattern, which involves sensory acuity and the flexibility to change. It is concerned with *differences* – what is the person doing differently that results in their behaviour and success, or failure? In other words, what is *the difference that makes the difference?* It does not attempt to answer the question *why*, but rather *how*. In this sense the technique is most pragmatic. Philosophers and theorists might eventually answer the why questions, but if modelling works, and we achieve our outcomes, our goal is already accomplished.

The process first involves, in effect, 'getting into the other person's shoes', or 'under their skin' – whatever metaphor you choose. This is a second person perceptual shift in NLP jargon, but it just means thinking the way you would if you were the other person – receiving rather than giving a communication, for instance, responding to an event or circumstance, or carrying out a behaviour or skill that you would like to be able to do yourself. We do it whenever we feel real empathy – 'I know just how you must have felt'. And it is a natural way to learn; you watch somebody, imagine yourself doing what they do, then have a go. Often the person you are modelling is not aware of how they are doing what they do (let alone why they have been blessed with their talents) so their strategies of thinking and behaviour will have to be elicited. Remember that excellence involves *unconscious* competence, so it should be no surprise that top performers are no more aware of just what they are doing, at least in a specific or micro sense, than anyone else.

Continuous improvement

Once you can achieve roughly the same results that your model achieves, making allowance perhaps for the extra years of experience they have, the next stage is to make changes until you arrive at the best strategy *for you*. By removing elements of the strategy and observing what difference it makes, you can eliminate strategies that are not contributing to your skill and results. If removing an element (to give simple examples, say taking three deep breaths before you tee off on the golf course, or thinking of your graduation ceremony before starting your speech) makes a big difference to your performance, you know it is a key to your success, and you may want to build on that strategy, again looking for the difference that makes the difference. This is the idea of continuous improvement – not of external products and systems, but in personal performance.

Communicating to others

The modelling process then extends to communicating your skills to others, and this is a feature that is important to managers and trainers. The language of NLP in terms of modalities (sensory representation systems) and submodalities (their qualities and specific characteristics) makes the process of acquiring excellent behaviours feasible and quite predictable. It makes it possible to compress into a short period the many years of trial and error experience that usually accompany excellence.

The early NLP models were examples of excellence in their field, even on a world-wide level. But this is not to suggest that NLP just applies to acquiring outstanding skills. Any behaviour – excellent or otherwise – can be modelled. For example, you might just want to read more quickly, be a better chairperson, or be more creative, and not win any contests at all. That is your choice. Having said that, excellence, in any field you like, is just a different strategy, and we can model it as easily as we can mediocrity. So once you have an understanding of strategies and the modelling process, you may find that your horizons are extended and you become dissatisfied with your present behaviour and achievements – which is no more than the natural human tendency to strive towards bigger and better purposes.

There is no mystique in this. Modelling just means drawing on what behaviour or way of thinking works for yourself and others, and using it to improve what you do. In Chapter 10 we looked at examples of how we run different meta programs which make us unique and account for the fact that there are such wide differences in personal achievement. If you think that being more positive – thinking in terms of what you want, rather than what you don't want – will help you get your outcomes, you can find someone who uses such a 'program'. Or if you want to measure yourself less against external criteria and more by what you feel inside, again you should be able to find people whom you can model. Eliciting these strategies means watching, listening and if need be, asking. Does the person use particular words or figures of speech? How do they express things they want? How do they walk, sit, talk to people, enter the boss's room? How do they imagine things? What are the pictures, or sounds, or feelings like? Do they talk to themselves? What sort of voice can they hear? What do they hear or say? The scope for modelling is endless, as it can be directed at these macro levels – say modelling a supreme optimist, or a super-creative person – or applied to very specific behaviours, say concerning manual skills, special communication situations at work such as disciplinary inter-views, or any sport. In each case there will be physiology, predicates (the words and phrases used) and representation systems (the pictures, sounds and feelings inside) involved. Some strategy characteristics are obvious, like body posture and the words we use. Some will need sensory acuity on your part to spot them. Others will need specific eliciting – you will have to ask the right questions, as the person may not be 'conscious' of what they are doing, especially in the mind. Check back to Chapter 6, where I listed some common submodalities, or characteristics of the main representation systems. These will help you to understand not just the richness of experience that you will discover when you model other people's personal perceptual maps, but simple lines of questions that will elicit a strategy: 'Did you see anything? What was it like? Big or small? Was it in colour? What sort of colours? Were your looking as if through your own eyes, or were you looking at yourself?' And so on. Refer back to the submodality list, but be ready for different descriptions of subjective experience that don't fit your or anyone else's model.

In the next chapter we will cover personal effectiveness strategies further, so that you can apply your modelling knowledge in any work or non-work situation. Just a reminder at this stage that everything you have learnt so far *still counts* – the importance of clear goals, the principles and techniques of effective communication, the four-part success model, and especially the presuppositions I outlined in Chapter 3. Modelling is the vehicle we use to understand and copy examples of excellence we can use in our own lives.

15

Strategies for Success

EARLIER, we discussed an important principle: 'The map is not the territory.' Our different perceptions of the world are reflected in different strategies that control our thoughts and behaviour. Just as corporate strategy is designed to achieve the company's goals or mission, so we have individual strategies to achieve our own outcomes.

We all have strategies, whether we are conscious of them or not, and whether they are effective or not. For instance, we have a personal strategy for motivation, for tidying our desk, for getting up for an early appointment, for getting rid of unwanted visitors, and so on. Although most of us enjoy some level of success, having got to where we now are in our complex lives, strategies can still, however, be identified, that work *better*.

Corporate strategy

What is the corporate equivalent? Organisational strategies are often in the form of written documents or phrases on framed statements along corridors. But even companies without declared strategies have them. You can detect it as you walk around the offices and plant, just as you can elicit from an individual person's behaviour what their main outcomes and values are. In other words, a strategy will be revealed by what we do – in a company, perhaps emphasising quality, low cost, high risk or low risk, the importance of people or of technology, and so on. A one-man enterprise or small company may have no formal document, but will operate a competition-beating strategy all the same, just as an individual operates unconscious but effective 'programs'. The job then is to know what these strategies are, largely adopted and perfected by default rather than by design, and to see what happens when we change them.

The syntax of success

The cooking or baking analogy is a good one to describe strategies. First there are the ingredients, which are like the representation systems we use – the sights, sounds and feelings that go to make up an experience, whether internally imagined or in the real world. Then we have to get the amounts right, and this is akin to the submodalities, rather like the adjustments on a television set; the amount of brightness or contrast, the volume and so on. Finally, as any good cook will tell you, you have to add the ingredients in the right order. This is the *sequence* of the steps we adopt to achieve something. We have already met this at a macro level, noting that some people need to *know* before they *do* or *get*, for instance. In fact the sequence, or syntax of a strategy, applies also at the lowest level of detail. These three factors – what to do, to what degree, and in what order – apply to strategies, and to successful modelling.

The modelling process

Otherwise the process is simple. Choose what you want to become better at, and choose an appropriate model who does the activity well. Then get the person to think back to when they carried out the behaviour, just as you recalled memories earlier and produced the feelings they originally evoked. What did they do first? What next? Specifically, what sights, sounds and feelings were involved (representation systems) and in what quantity or quality (submodalities)?

Let's say they are doing mental arithmetic. What exactly happens? Do they for example, see numbers? If so, how big are they, where do they appear in space, what colours are they? Are there neon lights or is there a blackboard? And so on. In one actual case the person described to me precisely how he saw the numbers, the specific colours of them, and explained how numbers that he found easy to manipulate were in primary colours or were bright, whilst difficult numbers were in sickly, pasty colours. In fact it was a fascinating inner word that was very familiar to the person and obviously the secret of his special skill.

What about sounds? In some cases people hold a dialogue, and the process involves language and voices, in the way we might recite a multiplication table to get at the right answer. Then there are feelings. An outcome or solution may have to *feel* right, and this feeling will need to be elicited in terms of its modalities and submodalities. A real physical feeling, or a sensation? Which sense, and what are the characteristics of the sense? There is usually a process involved for anything complex like arithmetic or spelling, and all three main representation systems may be involved. So the syntax, or order is vital. Did they start with a voice-like instruction, followed by whatever pictures were involved, then by the feeling of rightness? Or was there a running commentary while the pictures were happening? This is the difference that makes the difference, so the modelling process has to be probing and comprehensive, or you might miss the crucial strategies that result in success.

Eliciting chosen strategies

In carrying out this process you will need sensory acuity. You may not get neat answers to your questions – it is more likely that you will receive only vague descriptions or puzzled expressions. So you will need to interpret answers by paying attention to non-verbal clues, such as eye accessing cues (see Figure 6 in Chapter 9) which, once you are familiar with them, will prove more reliable than spoken responses. Or you can use the Meta Model, which is a powerful language tool to get more specific understanding of the deep structure of what is being said. If the person 'doesn't know' what happened next, adding perhaps that 'it just seems clear to me', but looks upward, the chances are they are accessing internal sights. Gentle questions such as 'What can you see that makes it clear?' usually move the process along. Eye access movement up and to the right will indicate a constructed image, which is consistent of course with seeing the desired outcome, rather than recalling a memory.

Coding strategies

Before discussing some specific strategies, a word about notation. V (visual) A (auditory) and K (kinaesthetic) are used when describing representation systems. This is followed by a superscript e denoting an external sense, so hearing, say, a real church bell would be A^e; i denotes an internal representation, so imagining what it feels like to swim in a cool lake would be K^i; and id denotes internal dialogue. The subscript c denotes a constructed image or sound, so imagining what a male friend would look like without his beard would be described as V^i_c.

Using this notation, any strategy can be recorded. For example, using the mental arithmetic example, but simplified, inner dialogue instructing the 'sum', followed by pictures of the numbers, followed by a feeling of rightness would be coded: $A^{id} > V^i > K^i$.

A motivation strategy is important, as this represents a person's 'hot button', so I will illustrate how these can differ, and the corresponding notation. Let's say that you start by looking at what has to be done, then constructing a mental picture of the finished job or task, followed by the happy feeling of having accomplished it, after which you tell yourself to get started. This will be described as $V^e > V^i_c > K^i > A^{id}$. One person, after looking at the task, asked himself what would happen if he did not do it, constructing (this time) *negative* images, and feeling bad enough to get started on the job. The syntax of his motivation strategy would be described: $V^e > A^{id} > V^i_c > K^i$. So not only can you arrive at your own motivation strategy in this way, but the universal coding allows you to compare what you do with others in a structured way. You can try changing the syntax, or order, of what you do. You can adapt strategies that work well for others, changing one variable at a time until you know what parts of the strategy are useful for you. What I have illustrated for motivation will also apply to creativity, feeling calm, or having courage. We have strategies for all our behaviour and states of mind.

Specific strategies

In the case of motivation, it soon becomes obvious that there is no right way or wrong way, and two people who demonstrate expert skills may apply quite different strategies. However, in the case of more specific applications, such as spelling or mental arithmetic, certain patterns may be common and thus give us standard strategies that we can apply without individual modelling – that is, you can draw on the strategies of 'good spellers' generally.

Spelling

This is a good example to take, partly because good spellers tend to adopt a similar strategy, and also because a lot of NLP work has been done in the area, including with people who are dyslexic. Because of the way we initially learn to spell, speaking out letters and words, and the emphasis on sounds, you would expect people with auditory senses to do well. This is not the case, however; spelling relies mainly on visual skills. In fact, poor spellers turn out to be those who try to rely on the sound of the word. The best spellers report seeing an image of the word and it feels familiar, or right. So here is a well-proven strategy, which, if you are not already using it, could make you a better speller:

1. Look at the word you want to remember how to spell for a few moments.
2. Look away from the word, then, moving your eyes up and to the left, visualise the spelling, looking back at the original image (in the book or wherever) to fill in any missing letters and correct any part of the word, repeating the process until you can easily visualise the proper spelling in your mind. It may help to place the image up and to your left, a little away from you, and you may want to imagine the word written in felt pen on a flip chart, or on a blackboard on chalk, or maybe in big plastic sign letters – find a system that has impact and makes it easy to remember.
3. Look away again, look up at you mental image, and write the word down. If it is not correct, go back to step 1, and do the short process again.
4. Try looking at your mental image and reading off the spelling backwards (something that is just about impossible to do phonetically).

There are other tips you can follow. You can break down longer words into convenient parts so that you are just spelling two or three short words. Even the longest word becomes manageable in this way. Just be sure you can see the whole word together. As well as imagining real writing, such as on a whiteboard, blackboard or flip chart, you can make the image a movie and actually write the words – seeing and feeling yourself writing with the marker pen, perhaps, and even hearing the noise of the pen on paper, or chalk on the blackboard. This brings the thing to life and makes it more memorable. Imagine using a colour you like. Imagine doing it in an environment you are confident in – perhaps on the kitchen wall, or drawing the words in the wet sand at a favourite beach, rather than risk negative connotations of school from your visualisation.

You can go a stage further and try to match the actual submodalities of memories from other areas you are good at (perhaps learning a game, or sport, or remembering cooking ingredients). In this case go back to the submodalities checklist to see the sort of characteristics that apply to your empowering memory, then switch them one by one to the spelling situation. But even without employing all the winning submodalities, changing to the basic visual strategy usually transforms a poor speller immediately.

Modelling practice

Why not do some work of your own on the other skill that sits alongside spelling – mental arithmetic? Find someone who does it well and find out how they do it. Do they see the numbers? What do they look like? Are they different colours, and what does this mean to the person? Does each number feel different? And how do they feel what they feel? Any sounds? And so on. Again, refer back to your submodalities checklist in Chapter 9 if you need to. Bear in mind that, as with spelling, you are likely to find different strategies, although you may well find common features in what is, essentially, a memorising exercise. Give each strategy a try. Even if something doesn't make sense it might well prove to be the key to a new skill for you. In some cases you will just need to amend what you are doing already, perhaps adding some weight to another modality, or 'tuning up' sound and picture controls here and there. In other cases you might have to abandon what you have been accustomed to doing as you find a patently better way of doing it. In each case you will need a period of practice before the new program becomes a habit, and your new competence becomes unconscious.

Creativity

Another strategy that has received a lot of attention is creativity. Walt Disney is renowned world-wide for his creative work, and Robert Dilts, a leading NLP writer and trainer, has created a model of his successful strategy, which I will describe. In this model the emphasis is on the different aspects of our personality, which from time to time will display creativity, and at other times a more realistic or critical aspect. The idea of inner parts is important in NLP – the different but positive intentions these parts have, the possibility of conflict and ineffectiveness if they are not working together, and the potential for excellence when they work in unity.

Let me illustrate this as it might apply to you as a manager. Whilst we may not all see ourselves as super-creative, we can usually think back to occasions when we acted creatively. In fact the very subconscious nature of this part of our thinking means that we usually surprise ourselves with the remarkable ideas we come up with. The problem is often that our more rational, realistic or critical part (the left brain) quickly makes its argument and our creativity is suppressed, and may never be given proper consideration. The real problem is, of course, that we need to be both realistic *and* critical at some point, so that our ideas can be turned into reality. Each part has a distinctive role to play, and each is less effective without the other.

Group creativity

In a group situation the same sort of problem occurs. A person may come up with a creative contribution, only to have it quashed by well-meaning critical or realistic voices. The culture this creates is one in which, pretty soon, good ideas are no longer voiced. So within an organisation a vast resource of personal creativity is wasted, as 'left brain' rationale, supported by convincing language (the speciality of the left brain) wins the day. Edward de Bono, a prolific author who coined the term *lateral thinking*, uses the idea of wearing different coloured hats to denote a particular thinking mode, so that in a group situation it becomes easier to think in a different way. All the views can be considered, including the far-fetched creative ones.

The application of this is even more appropriate at an individual level, in which the creative part may not even have the benefit of an impartial chairman, and because some of these parts (the creative rather than critical ones) may operate somewhere below consciousness, their contribution can go untapped.

—————————— EXERCISE ——————————

The Disney strategy

The Disney strategy involves three 'characters' or roles, giving each of them an opportunity to make their contribution.

1. Think of a situation or issue you would like to handle effectively. Make sure it is a real one – perhaps a personnel matter at work, a task which is complex and risky, or even intractable, or an opportunity you want to exploit – so that you give the technique a real test. Then allot three imaginary places in front of you which you can step into to represent your *dreamer*, your *realist*, and your *critic*.

2. First, think of a time when you were really creative, and you came up with plenty of new ideas and choices. You can think back to earlier jobs, or to non-work situations. Step into the dreamer position and relive the experience. As in previous techniques, go through each modality then bring the sights, sounds and feelings together so that you become what you then were. The place you step into simply anchors that experience. If you cannot think of a time when you were creative, put yourself in the shoes of someone you know who is, and imagine what they would feel like. Then step back from the creative position.

3. Next, think back to a time when you were realistic, careful

and well-organised. Perhaps when you put a plan into action, handling the many practical aspects effectively. You can similarly draw on your imagination of others who display this strength. When the experience is vivid, step into the realist position, anchoring your state to that physical spot, then step back out.

4. Finally, become your critic, thinking back to a time when you made constructive criticism, spotting the weakness in the arguments or solution. If you find this difficult, there is probably no shortage of critical people you could imagine thinking like. Step into the critic place, fully relive and anchor the experience, and step out again.

5. Now you have anchored these three states in the different locations, you can start to consider your problem. Step into your dreamer position and come up with all the creative ways you can imagine to solve the problem. Don't be side-tracked by what is feasible or sensible – just let the ideas flow unheeded, calling on the empowering creative state you have just experienced. In this state there is no criticism or even evaluation, so no idea will be put down. You can use language patterns such as 'What if . . .', 'I wonder if . . .', imagining what you might come up with if you were guaranteed success. This can be a pleasant experience, so enjoy your daydreaming, and get to know your creative location just like a favourite chair or room. When you have exhausted your creative ideas, step out of the position.

6. Then step into the realist position, and put your ideas into action. Think of all the practical considerations, timing, resources, things you will have to organise and initiate, until the ideas make sense. Ask yourself 'How can I do this?', and answer your own question in a pragmatic, realistic way. Then step back out of the position.

7. Next, step again into the critic position and this time use your critical skills to come up with all the snags. What have you forgotten? What might go wrong? What is the payback? Don't pull any punches, be as critical as you like, while staying constructive and always bearing in mind your outcome – the problem you are solving. Then step back into a neutral position.

8. Now return to your dreamer place, to think of more good ideas, this time addressing the practical problems and criticisms that have been made. Be just as creative in responding to barriers and shortcomings as you were when thinking of the initial ideas.

9. Continue to go through the cycle until your problem has been solved. You will probably find that one by one important weaknesses are solved – in effect becoming new problems – and that there is no limit to what your dreamer can think up when left to do the job without premature criticism. The critic will have fewer and fewer genuine criticisms but they will become more specific and can be addressed creatively. The realistic organiser will help to make each amended solution a practical reality. These three roles, whilst displaying strong identities of their own when anchored to their respective physical position, will begin to work more and more in harmony.

Note that the three roles work by addressing the problem, not confronting one another. So the realist and critic do not demean the dreamer, and the dreamer does not resent the criticism, creatively addressing the criticism rather than the critic. Most of us know what it is to criticise ourselves unduly, and this can indeed be destructive to our self-image and ineffective in terms of outcomes.

Inner partnership

The Disney creativity model shows how there is always a place for unhindered creativity, as well as for realism and criticism, in any situation. Creativity utilises the right brain, which is waiting to be harnessed in every one of us. It helps to explain the remarkable success of the Disney organisation, and is of course just one example of NLP modelling.

The potential applications for the strategy are wide. In Disney's case it could apply to a whole process, spanning months or years. But it can also be applied to a single issue, say concerning an individual member of staff. It can be used in a personal, DIY way, in pairs, or in a group situation. The advantage of involving more than one person is that the various contributions of the roles can be scribbled down as they are spoken, so that no ideas are lost in the process.

Changing states

For a critical manager, what may also be fascinating is to observe the different physiology displayed as a person goes from one state to the other. The body posture and tone of voice for instance, can change from one moment to the next as each state is anchored. This can be a revelation for someone who thinks they are not creative, or are not realistic, or no good at organising, as they start to display new skills. You can adapt the model – for example, at home you might use different rooms, or chairs – and to some extent at work. But observe the important NLP principles:

- Have an anchor – preferably a tangible, physical one – for each state, so that you can associate with it immediately, and build up that association over time, just like a favourite chair in which you can relax.
- Come out of one state before you enter another – another reason to use separate locations. There is otherwise the danger of taking one state with you to another, trying to wear more than one hat, which is where the difficulty started.
- Practise, just as with any skill, and be flexible. Apply the model to different kinds of problems, whether to do with people, processes, the short-term, the long-term.

These are just models and devices, and in practice you are free to think any way you want to think, and to change your point of view at will. So aim to be able to switch to one mode or another in an instant, say when taking part in a meeting or when confronted with an emergency situation. Imagining you are entering your room or other location, or sitting on a certain chair, for instance, can create the same association that physical changes can. Developing these empowering anchors is an important part of the learning process.

Strategy levels

This model also illustrates the different levels to which a strategy can apply. We saw when considering the Life Contents model that we can have an overriding tendency, say, to know things or get things, or to seek internal or external recognition. When thinking about spelling, however, more specific strategies were involved, so that the representations could be coded in a more detailed way using VAK notation.

Similarly, an individual strategy, say for motivation, memorising, or giving a speech, will also apply at any level of detail. There are books that cover each of these subjects in depth, and my book *The Right Brain Manager* has a chapter on memory. These books will give you a mixture of universal rules, akin to meta programs, and also the specific tips of the authors, based on their own strategies for success. Such specific strategies, for example, as elicited from the Disney brothers in the form of dreamer, realist and critic. Strategies, in effect, for

- coming up with off-the-wall ideas, perhaps involving relaxation, music and visualisation;
- for remembering practicalities, achieving targets, assessing resources, organising;
- generating constructive criticisms.

However, each person applying the Disney model is likely to use *different* strategies in each 'location' to do whatever they do. That is, any meta program, or model for creativity, pragmatism, or whatever will be supported by lower-level strategies, and indeed mixed up with other meta programs such as for motivation or optimism. The point is that, at whatever level, human behaviour is amenable to modelling. There are structures and strategies involved. A successful strategy will work again and again. By understanding the *structure* of experience, we can learn and benefit from each other. So empowering meta programs combine with specific strategies down to a micro level to produce mastery.

Modelling yourself

Some of the earlier references I made to modelling involved eliciting strategies from people whose excellence you want to emulate. The Disney model makes it clear, however, that we can draw on our own memories. Somewhere inside us we each have a dreamer, realist and critic that, given the right environment, can act with expertise and wisdom on our behalf. Thus we have already within us resources of competence that can be called upon to increase our effectiveness. If you have ever been highly motivated, ever been in a confident, resourceful state, ever been productive and industrious, ever been persuasive and compelling, you need not travel the world to find your models. Simply switch one successful strategy to another application. Sport to work. Office to home. Private to public and vice versa. Value a winning strategy for its own sake, regardless of the special circumstances – the content – that surrounded it. Just like a special recipe for a cake, or instructions to get to a street in Aberdeen, the strategy will work for anyone who is willing to understand it and stick to it. Personal effectiveness means finding strategies that work best – your own, or those of others – and discarding those that are not so effective in pursuing your goals.

From competence to excellence

We can change strategies of *competence*, to create strategies of *excellence*. As I said earlier, parts of our mental syntax can be removed to see what effect this has on outcomes. We can change modalities, for example using mental pictures when we used to concentrate on self talk, and changing – to any degree of detail we wish – the many submodalities involved. This is the individual pursuit of excellence. The process is one that top performers in all fields use, even without knowing what they are doing that brings their success. It is the familiar sensory acuity, flexibility success model we met right at the beginning. In terms of personal effectiveness there is probably more mileage for managers in understanding and using this model of learning and self awareness than in acquiring more and more knowledge or specific skills. The appropriate knowledge needed will soon become clear as we strive for success in outcome terms, and individual skills (such as interviewing, public speaking, listening, problem solving, etc.), will follow as strategies of 'unconscious competence'. Remember that the strategies we have been discussing tend to operate at an unconscious level, once we have got through the initial learning, and this is where effectiveness lies.

Understanding and applying models for strategy change is the essence of so-called accelerated learning. We can speed up the natural and usually inefficient process of learning by experience, by drawing on more successful strategies, that we operate at other times or in other situations, or by drawing on the experience of others, however apparently unreachable their level of proficiency. Provided we are willing to use both sides of our brains, or more aptly harness our many inner parts, we all have the hardware we need to bring about extraordinary achievements. NLP gives structure, technique and predictability to this process.

◀ PART FIVE ▶

Creative Problem-Solving

16

Thinking with Both Sides of Your Brain

THE manager is a professional problem-solver. If you don't consider this to be so, maybe you have missed something – there are perhaps a couple of problems you are not yet aware of. In terms of outcomes, the 'problem' is getting from one state to another – from A to B, as in the change of state model we met in Chapter 4. The same principle applies to opportunities, which can also be termed 'problems'. Even a windfall opportunity has to be turned into reality – and that is your problem. You will certainly have a problem if you *miss* opportunities, or threats. I use the term 'problem' quite positively, in terms of changing your state (from A to B), achieving outcomes, and making possible what seems impossible.

Managers are usually practical and pragmatic, being concerned with outputs, performance and bottom lines. In terms of problem definition, and deciding on the outcome you want, rather than what you don't want, the principles we covered in Part Two are all very applicable. The various tests of a well-formed outcome ensure that our goal, and the problem gap it represents, is well defined. As in the case of goals, we can consider problem-solving from the two-brain perspective – logically and analytically, and intuitively and imaginatively. Each contributes to the holistic, or whole-brain approach needed for complex problems in a rapidly changing environment and in the face of strong competition.

Various problem-solving models are well covered in other management texts. Typically, the process is divided into problem-definition and decision-making. The process involves:

- *recognising* the problem, which includes both awareness and any facts or opinions involved;
- *labelling* – an agreed, more precise statement of the problem;
- *analysis* – typically finding and agreeing on the main source of the problem.

The decision, or solution part includes:

- a complete listing of possible *options*;
- *evaluation* – choosing the best solution so that a firm (possibly joint) decision can be made;
- a step-by-step *action plan* for bringing the solution to reality.

This sort of process, which will be familiar to managers, applies to just about any type and size of problem, although timescales vary a lot, of course. I am concerned here with those problems that NLP can particularly help with. We have already seen some NLP presuppositions which slot easily into the above model:

- the importance of setting precise outcomes, or clearly defining your problem;
- the need for choices; and
- the importance of action.

This sort of model, as well as being used as a systematic, group or organisational basis for problem-solving, also reflects the thinking involved. There are several stages in the thought processes involved in solving a problem, or in carrying out a task or project involving problems and decisions. This is not an NLP model, but will help to bridge the gap between some conventional problem-solving approaches that will be familiar to managers, and a more creative, holistic approach, where NLP can certainly help. In particular, I will show the importance of unconscious thought processes in goal achievement and decision-making. Also in this part, after describing these thinking stages, and some important aspects of problem-solving, I will cover the important NLP topic of reframing, or seeing things from different points of view. This introduces a major creative perspective to otherwise rational but not always effective techniques and systems. I will then describe some specific NLP techniques that have been used successfully by managers in business and personal problem-solving. Finally, in this part I will describe how these approaches can apply to some specific, conventional problem-solving methods with which you are likely to be familiar.

THINKING STAGES

It may be useful to see thinking in terms of stages. These are not necessarily sequential, but the model illustrates the way different mental 'operating' systems seem to be at work. The model also helps to relate individual thought processes with the more familiar stages in executing a task or managing a project.

Preparation

Preparation relates to the planning stage in a task or project, and includes problem definition, data gathering and making any assumptions. It is closely linked to the first stage in the four-part success cycle we met in Part One, when you decide exactly what you want – your outcome. Writing down your problem statement (labelling), and using visualisation techniques to see the desired outcome can be incorporated successfully into specific problem-solving, as well as goal-setting.

The corporate equivalent of thinking preparation can involve quite elaborate planning and project systems, and agreeing on mission statements and strategies. But for shorter-term or *ad hoc* problems, this stage, although a good investment of time and resources, is often overlooked or cut short. The type and degree of preparation will depend of course upon the nature and size of the problem. But each thinking stage is important.

We saw earlier the importance of having an outcome for a communication, and this is part of the problem-solving preparation. What exactly do I want to achieve? The communication 'problem', of course, as with any outcome you want to achieve, is to bridge the gap between present state and desired state, be it to inform, persuade, question, or whatever.

Horses for courses in planning

A telephone call may require no more than a scribbled note listing the key points you have to cover, and the purpose or end result of the call. A similar process, taking seconds or a few minutes, will also apply to memos, faxes, and many other day-to-day communications. A major report, on the other hand, may require a whole day, or long uninterrupted periods for proper preparation, including the definition of your aims, the resources or information you need, and the design and structure of the document itself.

In each case, both left and right brain will be called into play. Logical analysis and written notes, bullet points and summaries are obvious left-brain functions. Visualising your desired outcome (such as the result of your telephone call, the acceptance and implementation of your report, a happy customer) adds a right-brain dimension. Intuitive judgement, which we will meet in later thinking stages, may also help your preparation – a leap of intuition might tell you 'This is not the real problem, but so and so is', or some other 'Aha!'-type revelation.

Size and ecology

There is another way to approach this problem. At this stage also, and this was covered in the outcome tests, you may have to adjust the size of the problem – perhaps breaking it down into manageable chunks. By addressing the problem in sequential stages you may be able to tackle it better. Conversely, by chunking it up, seeing it as perhaps a bigger or more general problem, or in a wider context, you may get a more holistic view of the situation.

Ecology, as we described in the outcome tests, may come into it. You may put all your effort into what you think is the 'problem' (say designing a filing system) when the *real* problem (perhaps to do with personal time management, organisation structure, or some aspect of communication), of which you are not consciously aware, continues unrecognised and may negate any brilliant solution you come up with. That is, there are conflicting outcomes. This is a factor that is better considered before, rather than in the middle of your task, when energy has already been expended.

Look on the preparation stage as a high-dividend investment. It is not just about the time you put in – as I have said, in some cases just a few moments are needed. It concerns the quality of thought that clearly defines outcomes and is open to creative insights.

Analysis

This is where you look at the problem in depth, considering all the angles, the pros and cons, the implications. Many conventional problem-solving approaches are restricted to this familiar activity, in which the conscious thinking brain is put to work in an orderly way. Analysis, or considering parts rather than the whole, is associated with the left brain. The process is a linear, sequential one; one step follows another. Logical argument may be used: 'If so and so . . . then so and so'.

Unfortunately, the further you go down one of these logical paths, the more you are committed to it, and the less chance there is of coming up with an entirely different line of thinking. The advantage is that such thinking is amenable to methods and systems, so can become standardised within organisations and will form part of a manager's normal delegation of responsibilities. The disadvantage is that most problems that find their way to the manager's desk have already been addressed by sound logical thinkers, or have been subject to 'systems' or computer programs. It is the tricky, insoluble ones, often with a large 'people' element, that the manager is paid to solve.

Sequential and lateral thinking

It is important to understand the limitations of analytical problem-solving, and to know when creative thinking is needed. As an example, consider the diagram in Figure 9. The problem is to make a familiar geometric shape using the cardboard shapes given at each stage. The illustration shows the typical solution. Unfortunately, as you can see, the final shape cannot be accommodated.

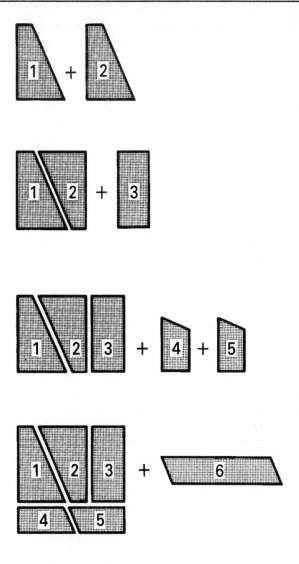

FIGURE 9 Left-brain sequential thinking

Figure 10 (see page 183) shows an alternative solution, which does meet the requirement. In this case, instead of the more obvious square, a parallelogram is chosen, and this turns out to be acceptable in the eventual solution.

Creative thinking assumes there are infinite solutions, at every stage in a problem, and thus you stay more open to possibilities. This is important when, as in modern business life, we are confronted with new variables at every turn, goalposts tend to get moved, and earlier assumptions and conclusions no longer hold good. Ideally we should be ready to go back to 'square one' with every new piece of information or change in circumstances. Analytical, sequential problem-solving – the standard kind – renders this almost impossible. We don't usually re-think until we are completely stuck, having expended energy and resources, and maybe lost face.

The analysis stage can be taken to any lengths, as is illustrated by the tendency to perfectionism with many managers, and the proliferation of business schools developing new analytical models. The economic law of diminishing returns, however, is usually at work, and you don't usually get proportionate rewards for each successive amount of effort and time you put in. You can easily lose track of where you have got to and your initial problem. Sometimes you reach a point when you get frustrated and need to bring a fresh mind to the problem, or call a halt, which is the next stage in the thinking process.

Frustration

Few management textbooks admit to this stage, although most managers are more than familiar with it. This is when you come to a 'blank wall', feel you are 'going round in circles', or are ready to pack in altogether. It may come very soon after you have embarked on your problem-solving or task, or when you are well into it, but its effect is the same. You are tempted to throw in your hand, and get on with something that will produce more immediate results.

Paradoxically, frustration is an important part of the mental process. Some of the greatest thinkers in the world talk of going through serious periods of frustration, doubt or depression, when they are ready to throw in the towel. What they also testify to, however, is that out of this state some of their greatest insights and revelations have come. Outstanding discoveries are often born out of this stage in the process.

The body and mind, in fact, are giving an important message. The message is to let the issues go underground – that is, pass them to the subconscious mind for a different kind

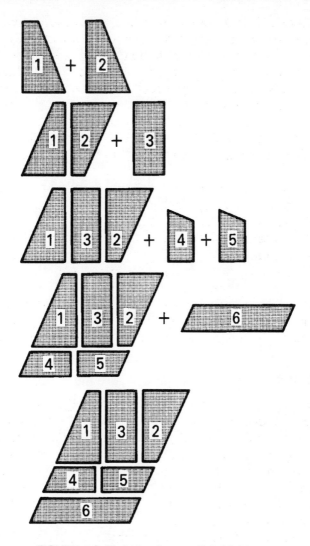

FIGURE 10 Right-brain parallel thinking

of processing. When you find yourself in this state you don't need to do anything about the problem in hand. It is usually counterproductive, and you become even more frustrated. Just do, or think about, something completely different. Start another task, tidy you desk, visit a colleague, walk round the park – do anything that will take your conscious mind off what you are doing for a while. Sleep on it.

Incubation

This is the passive period when things are right out of your conscious control. It is when we 'sleep on the problem'. The word incubation comes from the Latin root word for 'lying down'. And that is an ideal analogy – you stop trying, you relax, and put the problem out of your mind. Unlike the analysis stage which you can schedule and build into your diary, you cannot control the timing of this thinking stage. It has its own rules, but doesn't divulge them. You can't demand a flash of inspiration by five o'clock, or a eureka in time for the deadline the MD has given you. The incubation period can last for anything from a few moments to several years. If, for instance, you forget a name for a moment, the chances are that by changing the subject it will come to your mind within a couple of minutes. In other cases you may have been ruminating on a problem for weeks and a solution comes in the middle of the night, or at some other time when you least expect it. People talk about getting amazing eurekas which solve, in a moment, issues they have been tackling for years. In fact the incubation process has been going on below consciousness.

Sleep, and the dreaming process, are the ultimate examples of incubation and confirm the basic need we all have for this form of thought processing, even to live our day-to-day lives. How many times has a problem seemed less daunting, or even disappeared altogether, in the light of a new day?

The incubation stage runs counter to the work ethic, and is hard for active managers to accept. You lose control; you don't seem to be *doing* anything. But this is the natural, effective way to goal-achievement and problem-solving, and it will pay you to come to terms with this passive aspect of your problem-solving role.

In my research among top business leaders this aspect of thinking turned out to be a common feature. Many actually geared up their lifestyle to make time for relaxation and winding down, and their best thinking, usually resulting in solid bottom-line results, happened at these times. Later in this part of the book I will describe specific NLP techniques to get you into the state you decide is best for your purposes.

Insight

This is an enjoyable stage in the problem-solving process. Out of the blue an idea comes which takes you a lot further forward, and sometimes you get the solution on a plate. It is linked with right-brain intuition, insight, and the eurekas with which so many outstanding scientific advances are associated. It happens typically when your conscious mind is occupied with something completely different, and so can come as a surprise or shock to the system. As we have seen, it is more likely to come when you are relaxing or away from the office, than when you are fretting over the problem in question.

One manager woke in the middle of the night and proceeded to write, more or less word for word, an important report that had been troubling him for many weeks. Another solved a tricky people problem when mowing his lawn on a Sunday. NLP helps us to get in touch with these thinking 'parts' of us that contribute in different ways. We saw in the Disney model in Chapter 15, for instance, how you can get into a creative state just when you need to, and so increase the quality of your insight and the success of your outcomes.

Implementation

Eventually our ideas have to be changed into reality, and your solutions realised in real life. This stage is concerned with implementation of tasks and projects, and the pragmatic bottom line of the business. Subjective thought becomes objective reality, dreams become facts. Ideas are not much use if they don't have any effect on material outcomes; models, systems and theories have to pass the test of utility and benefit.

As we have seen, there are some parts of this process over which we have little control, when the unconscious mind is at work. However, it is possible to be more creative throughout all the stages and thus increase our problem-solving skills. We saw in the goals section the role of mental rehearsal, for instance, in fixing goals firmly, and their cybernetic effect in guiding us towards those goals. The insight stage can in fact happen at any time, anywhere. You may get an idea, for instance, during the preparation or problem-definition stage that changes the whole nature of the problem or task. In particular, assumptions may not always be supported by hard facts, and you may have to exercise lots of subjective judgement. Knowing what data are needed, and when you should call a halt, also requires a decision which no computer program can help you with and which may not have any logical basis. You will have to have a *feel* for the situation at every stage if you are not to go down blind alleys and miss opportunities. A short incubation can work wonders even at the initial preparation stage. Similarly an invaluable eureka can come when in the middle of detailed analysis. And you certainly need all the creativity you can get when implementing your solution or decision, confronting all the obstacles that the real world places in your path. These problem-solving stages are not watertight processes, but simply illustrate the way the holistic mind works on the most complex issue, drawing on the unconscious mind all the time.

Think of your biggest single problem, and subject it to the full cycle. Apply all the skill and effort the problem deserves and use every analytical technique you can find, but most of all, be aware of the need to stop trying at the appropriate time. Learn to harness your whole brain in a creative way, as we have seen. In the following section I will discuss further how creativity can be part of the whole problem-solving process.

LATERAL AND VERTICAL THINKING

The main distinction I want to make is between lateral, or creative thinking, and vertical, or logical, sequential thinking. Creative problem-solving means getting away from the usual linear, logical, perhaps more obvious approach, and being open to whatever other choices there may be.

The need to give special attention to creative thinking arises because of the way we naturally process thoughts. Sometimes we think of the brain as an information processing system like a filing system, library or computer. However, whereas in these cases (and indeed when we are consciously analysing any problem) we actively sort information into categories or patterns, in the mind this is done passively or automatically. The mind just creates an environment in which information, in effect, sorts itself, and we are largely unaware of the process.

The changing mental landscape

Our mental or perceptual 'map' is the result of a lifetime of self-organisation – one vast memory landscape of experiences and perceptions. A landscape is in fact a good analogy, because a natural landscape is also a memory surface, recording the accumulated 'experience' of rainfall, streams, rivers and erosion which have resulted in its present contours. And like the natural landscape, the human mind also works in a dynamic, plastic way in relation to the forces acting on it – the five senses.

As well as the rain changing the landscape, the landscape changes the course of the rain, which follows existing contours and so has a self-perpetuating influence. So it is with thinking. Once we have created convenient mental patterns or contours, any further sensual inputs will be affected by what has gone before – our background and experiences, beliefs and values. And the stronger the mental patterns, or the deeper the landscape of ravines and valleys, the more further sensory inputs will create even deeper contours.

The system is amazingly effective for adaptation and survival, being able to classify sensory stimuli unconsciously and allowing us to react instantly to a real and potentially dangerous outside world. But for higher thinking, it has its drawbacks. Sometimes historical mindsets lose their validity. The world changes, and so do our outcomes. Beliefs, however, tend to stay unchanged long past their sell-by date and have the same immutable effect on a sensory raindrop as the well-carved-out river gorge. Hence the enduring mindsets, prejudices, attitudes and values that do not support or empower us in our present interests.

Upsetting familiar mindsets

So our mental maps are not simple records of actual sensory experiences, any more than a natural landscape is simply a memory of pristine rain, sun and wind – in a large part these are both self-created. A memory, as Edward de Bono puts it, is 'anything that happens and does not unhappen', so the result is some trace that is left. And those billions of traces are what form our unique perceptual maps of the world, the unique patterns that we are convinced are real or 'right' and 'obvious'. Lateral thinking upsets these patterns, creates new contours, sees familiar things in a new light, and gives us choices about how we perceive and behave. That's the sort of thinking we need when the world around is changing, and yesterday's solutions no longer work.

As we have seen, we can think what we want to think, so this whole neural network is changeable – programmable – to achieve our outcomes. This is where the programming part of neuro-linguistic programming comes in. Reframing is a major part of NLP which attempts to get a different perspective on experience. This is vital for insight, judgement, and other such characteristics that managers accept are needed for personal effectiveness. In particular, it is a neglected but crucial aspect of problem-solving.

Comparing lateral and vertical thinking

Before addressing the subject of reframing, I will summarise the differences between lateral and what is termed vertical thinking.

- *Vertical thinking is selective; lateral thinking is generative.* Vertical thinking selects one route and rejects all others. Lateral thinking seeks to identify all possible routes, watching for new ones, and keeps any option open. Remember that 'Choice is better than no choice'.
- *Vertical thinking moves in discrete steps; lateral thinking can make logical jumps.* The logic can be filled in backward.
- *In vertical thinking you have to be correct at every step; with lateral thinking the end result is what is important.* Just as when building a bridge, the parts do not need to be self-supporting until the end. Compare this with the NLP emphasis on outcomes, and the cybernetic model of goal-achieving in which continuous route-finding is always directed towards a clear target.
- *Vertical thinking eliminates unpromising pathways, but there are no negatives with lateral thinking.*

Every path is potentially useful, even thought it may not appear so at the moment. Compare the positive requirement of a well-formed outcome, and the presupposition 'There is no failure, only feedback.'

- *Vertical thinking is quick to apply labels and classify; lateral thinking avoids categorising or pattern-making.* The ubiquitous nominalisations we met in the Meta Model are examples of the tendency, in language and thinking generally, to generalise and conceptualise.

- *Vertical thinking follows the most likely path; lateral thinking will pursue the least likely.* Some of the specific reframing techniques later are designed to turn things a full 180 degrees around to get at a different meaning.

As we saw in the thinking stages above, real thinking power comes from a special partnership of these often diametrically opposed approaches, in which the two brain hemispheres specialise. But the different viewpoints give you choices, and choices can be translated into effectiveness. In the next chapter I will discuss further how you can generate more points of view, and thus choices, by reframing.

17

Reframing

THE idea of reframing is to see things from a different perspective, or within a different 'frame' or context. Reframing is the essence of creative thinking, and echoes earlier concepts such as lateral thinking. It fits squarely with some of the presuppositions we met at the outset. In order to understand other people's maps of reality, for instance, we need to be able to see things from their point of view, or 'get into their shoes', as we might say – the metaphor is not so important as the principle, which we saw is crucial to good communication. This generates choices, or opens possibilities, and, as we also saw, 'choice is better than no choice'. An open, receptive approach is more likely to identify the important intentions which underlie behaviour, but which might not fit our own perceptions of what is right or sensible. All of this brings better understanding, better communication, and it achieves goals.

Context and content reframing

Any behaviour, situation, or event can be reframed. Just by changing the context, for instance, new meanings are likely to be generated. To take an extreme example, getting down on all fours and barking like a dog could be career-limiting for a senior manager; but the same behaviour when he is playing with his son at home is acceptable or even commendable. It is also fine on a Thursday night at the amateur dramatic society. Wearing jeans torn at the knees is now acceptable in all sorts of situations, but change the context, say to a job interview or board meeting, and the behaviour has a different meaning. This is known as *context reframing*.

But a behaviour can be reframed in any way you like, even keeping the context as it is. *Who* is wearing the jeans? A middle manager, the chairman, or an important client? Any part or aspect of the *content* of the situation can also change its meaning. A drop in gross margins might be bad news at the monthly management meeting. But the same set of figures might show record sales, improved cash flow, a reduction in overheads, and success at breaking into a new market that will bring big winnings in the future. The interpretation depends on what part of the content you focus on. Advertising is all about content reframing. Change the angle, focus on some aspect of it, and you change the meaning. Change the meaning, and you will change how you feel and behave – you have more choices.

Before introducing some reframing techniques, let me describe the idea of frames. The frame is the context into which we put things, and what gives them meaning. It is what makes the behaviour or situation important or unique to us. There are different ways of framing events, and it will become clear as these are illustrated.

Outcome frame

This is the frame we adopt when stressing the importance of outcomes, and making sure, according to several criteria, that they are well-formed. It is one way of considering behaviour; we might have considered just the effort put in (the effort frame), or the process rather than the outcome (the process frame). By adopting an outcome frame, say in a meeting or negotiation, you will focus on the outcome you are after, and all your behaviour will be directed accordingly. Adopting such a frame not only enables you to be more effective in directing your own goal-achieving actions, but will identify the difference between your outcome and that of others, especially in negotiation, so that you can seek to constructively get agreement, in a win-win way. Having adopted this frame or reference, your 'problem', the gap between the two outcomes, is clearer and more likely to be solved. This is the frame that applies to the cybernetic model of goal-achievement, and when thinking in terms of outputs rather than inputs. By thinking in terms of outcomes, you will be aware of how far you are off target, so that you can amend your behaviour accordingly. MBO, management by objectives, popular a couple of decades ago, is another example of the outcome frame in practice in organisations. A so-called goal-oriented person 'frames' their life in terms of outcomes.

Ecology frame

We met this frame when describing the 'present state to desired state' outcome model. The 'journey' we make from one state to another, or the gap we bridge, is always within the frame of other outcomes and intentions; any reservations we have are likely to affect our outcome – we have got to *want* to bridge the gap, and have to believe that the outcome is both achievable and worthwhile. A single-minded person who pursues one goal regardless of its wider effect does not 'frame' his behaviour in terms of ecology. Ecology, you will recall, was also one of the tests of a well-formed outcome, raising the sort of question: 'Is my behaviour consistent with the wider interests of family, fellow professionals, and friends. Is it congruent with other goals I have?' Our outcome was within an ecology frame.

Evidence frame

You will recognise this one also as one of the outcome tests we applied. This concentrates on evidence, and the specific details of the outcome. It is part of the outcome frame, and will emphasise the sensory evidence of your outcome – what you will see, hear and feel. Sensory evidence is not all there is to goal-achievement, but it is an important frame of reference.

'As if' frame

This is particularly useful in problem-solving and is a feature of other more conventional techniques. You act 'as if' other conditions obtained, or other events occurred. It is akin to scenario planning: 'What if this happened?' or 'Let's suppose so and so.' You might not have the financial resources for a promising investment, but what if you had? You don't have the accountant's comments on the figures, but what might he say? You can apply the frame to time and think 'as if' an outcome has been achieved, then look back to imagine the way you got to where you are. This approach crops up in positive thinking books when we are asked to imagine the worst that could happen, mentally accept it, then do whatever we can to make things better. Insurance companies refer to 'downside planning'. More frequently 'best', 'worst' and 'probable' alternatives are worked out in planning and budgeting exercises. These are just different 'as if' frames.

Backtrack frame

In this case you re-present information you have received from someone, perhaps in a meeting, as a way of gaining agreement and commitment about what has gone before. Rather than being a chairperson's synopsis, it is a genuine attempt to recapitulate on what has been communicated. It is a vital tool in negotiation, often being used repeatedly to ensure ongoing agreement. It is a good rapport tool, as it shows you are listening and that you understand what is being communicated. It is often characterised by phrases such as: 'Now let me be sure I have got this right', 'So this is where we have got to . . .', or 'Correct me if I'm wrong, but . . .'. In some cases a more formal backtrack will be used in meetings based on an actual transcript.

The concept of reframing should now be clear. By adopting another frame, and the above are just a few common examples, you will gain a new perspective on things and a better understanding. Even more fundamentally, until we *give* things a frame, they have little importance to us – they don't *mean* anything. We give things meaning according to our individual perceptual filters based on our family, cultural or educational background. This is part of the brain's sophisticated classification system which serves us well in most situations. For new situations and change, however, we need to break out of familiar mindsets, and reframe our experience to get new, more useful interpretations. That is what creative thinking is all about, and a creative, reframing approach to problem-solving will give you a head start over conventional, more blinkered thinkers.

An anecdote, metaphor or simile, the punch line of a joke, a facet or new angle on a subject, a twist in the meaning; these are no more than popular forms of reframing. There are outstanding historical examples, such as when Einstein went for a ride on an imaginary beam of light, putting a different frame on his blackboard mathematics, and coming up with his theory of relativity. Reframing is just a fancy term for figures of speech and concepts we use all the time, but in problem-solving we have hardly begun to know its effect.

SLEIGHT OF MOUTH

There are various techniques that can help us reframe. The so-called Sleight of Mouth pattern (referring to the conjuror's sleight of hand), which I have adapted and used both in groups and as a DIY tool, is a popular NLP model. This considers a statement from different points of view. Although the angles are 'standardised', typically scores of different angles can be generated, so it is an effective problem-solving tool. Unlike traditional brainstorming, you do not need to get a group together, as any single, standard brain can generate highly creative points of view with appropriate stimulation. The points of view include respectively positive and negative, an overall or general view, and a more focused perspective, as well as a more personal or value-based perspective.

Here is a problem statement I once heard, that might have come from any manager in any type or size of organisation:

> *'You can't empower people in our*
> *short-term, results culture.'*

The following are the Sleight of Mouth points of view, and examples of the responses they might generate to the problem statement.

Positive outcome

'So you agree we need to work on the culture also?'
'You've obviously been giving this serious thought.'
'At least the staff are measured on merit.'
This looks for a silver lining in the dark cloud.

Negative outcome

'So morale will continue to fall?'
'You don't think we can turn round the production numbers, then?'
'Will we lose the best staff?'
This is the downside, or maybe worst-case scenario.

A different or further outcome

'Could we get to see the regional director next month?'
'What about extending the middle management training programme?'
'It's not so much the culture, but the chairman.'
'It's just a matter of getting through the recession.'
Another outcome, which may well affect the problem statement's implied outcome, is suggested.

A metaphor

'Have you ever heard of people eating their own seedcorn.'
'There are so many round pegs in square holes.'
'It's like pruning your roses in a rainstorm.'
'Oil and water just don't mix.'
A story, simile or anecdote might suffice. The metaphor does not provide a solution, but stimulates the problem-stater's unconscious mind to come up with his own reframe. The metaphor does not have to make *sense* – the sense comes from any useful association it triggers.

A different timescale

'Let's see how it is after Christmas.'
'Has it got any worse over the last year?'
'How long have you got to retirement?'
The time factor is reframed as an added perspective.

A model of the world

'I suppose we live in an imperfect world.'
'Results are what modern business is all about.'
'Things don't get simpler, do they?'

This is the bird's-eye view, wide-angle perspective, or philosophical view of the situation.

Personal values and criteria

'Are you telling me you're not empowered?'
'Don't you agree that the business results come first?'
'Does that give you a problem personally?'
'How do you cope with that situation?'
This focuses the problem at a personal level, eliciting possible attitudes and values that might be involved.

Redefine

'Maybe they don't want to be empowered.'
'Maybe we need to go for more automation.'
'Perhaps we are not getting the right message across.'
The problem itself is redefined.

Chunk up

'Is it an industry-wide problem?'
'Do you have difficulty with your people generally?'
'Nobody seems to think ahead.'
The problem is lifted to a higher, more general level, giving a wider perspective.

Chunk down

'Who is giving you the trouble?'
'What about your immediate team?'
'How is recruitment affected?'
This focuses on a part of the problem, which might well hinge on a detail.

Counter-example

'What about Joe in sales?'
'XYZ plc have managed to devolve their management.'
Counter-examples sometimes are in the form of 'Ah, but . . .'.

Positive intention

'It sounds as though you are concerned about the firm's future.'

'So you are keen to influence this short-termism?'
'You've been trying to give your staff more freedom?'
This attempts to elicit a positive *intention* (rather than outcome) on the part of the problem-holder.

You will see that each point of view is a quite familiar way of looking at things, so no super creativity is called for. You will probably have used each of them yourself from time to time. The model, however, forms a useful and powerful checklist, and will especially prevent us from sticking to our own comfortable ways of seeing things. If you start to think laterally, any number of examples or responses will come to mind, so you can easily generate scores of perspectives, any one of which may unlock your problem.

You will also note that although the points of view are used as a check-list, the questions or responses certainly don't come as standard. That's just what reframing is *not* about. If we are not to move from one limiting mindset to another using a neatly structured but blinkered approach, our personal creative thinking has to be stimulated.

New angles

Another important point to stress is that the responses should not attempt to solve the problem, but should simply open another angle on it which may well result in the problem-owner finding and *owning* his own solution. It is just as important to own a solution to a problem as to own the problem in the first place. A metaphor, anecdote, quotation, or saying, for instance, will have a certain meaning to one person and a different meaning to another – some of the above examples may have seemed a reasonable input to the problem and the others nonsense. A new perspective that is 'nonsense', or ridiculous, however, is more likely to create the vital change of mindset than one which is obvious and sensible. After all, you have applied the common-sense points of view already but still have a problem. Metaphors conjure sights, sounds and feelings, rather than words or concepts which may not stimulate the senses in the same way. So the chances are that some meaning will be got, even if it is different from what the responder may have intended. And even a tenuous association with the problem may be enough to trigger a new line of thought. Similarly, 'chunking down' need not focus on the precise part of the problem that might hold the key. It is the *process* of thinking in that more focused way that identifies a specific part of the problem that will make the difference. If the real problem is to do with the problem-holder, rather than the external circumstances or perhaps people involved, a response is unlikely to pinpoint the specific cause of the problem, which may be a certain attitude, hang-up, or prejudice – hence the personal or values perspective. Switching our thinking inwards, rather than suggesting what we think about, is what is likely to bring about the reframing. Each point of view can open up unlimited opportunities for a solution, in what logically may be an intractable situation.

Making associations

In each case it is the openness to any possible meaning that is the real strength of this reframing tool, rather than a clever technique. We constantly make associations between what we perceive in the world and our present map. These associations, which cannot of course be predicted or controlled, are what produce insightful, creative and effective solutions. The more sensory stimuli that create associations, the more chance there is of the winning association occurring. So aim for quantity in points of view, rather than clever stabs at a complete solution.

This is a flexible model. Add any other points of view you can think of. If you can't think of any responses, move on to another point of view. If you feel particularly comfortable about one or two of the patterns, think of as many questions or responses as you can. But bear in mind that a point of view that seems irrelevant or stupid may be the very one that unlocks a fixed mindset – which might be the real problem.

Sleight of Mouth can be used at a personal level, by two people, or on a group basis. Obviously more creative ideas will be generated by more people, but do not underestimate the more or less unlimited ability of one person to come up with astonishingly creative insights, given some mental stimulation.

POINTS OF VIEW

There is another simple reframing model, which uses the title Points of View. This uses common opposed pairs of words such as good and bad, right and wrong, etc. to generate different meanings. For example, we might say it is bad that there have to be layoffs. An opposed point of view using 'good' might be 'It is *good* that there will be layoffs, as we can at last move back into profit.' Or, 'It is *right* that there will be layoffs, as turnover cannot sustain present numbers.'

The words used in this model are:

good, bad, right, wrong, stupid, smart, better, worse.

As in any reframe, we start from where we are, and it helps to have a clear problem-statement. Points of View is particularly helpful in getting perspectives on personal or people problems. For example a common complaint about managers is 'He never listens'. Using the model, the following points of view might be generated:

It's *good* that he never listens *because* he would get too involved in the detail.

It's *bad* that he never listens *because* morale is getting worse.

It's *right* that he never listens *because* he is not responsible.

It's *wrong* that he never listens *because* we could avoid so many problems.

It's *stupid* that he never listens *because* he could save time and effort.

It's *smart* that he never listens *because* he doesn't worry over unnecessary details.

It's *better* not to listen *than* get bogged down with other people's work.

It's *worse* not to listen *than* not to understand.

The model is more restricted than the Sleight of Mouth, as you will need to fit the problem statement into the syntax of the pattern. It is, however, very useful for generating a variety of insights into 'people' problems like the example shown.

Creating choices

Once again, multiple alternatives can be generated from one trigger word in respect of a single problem. Have a go at applying this to any people problems you face as a manager. They can be as specific or as general as you like. Difficulty in thinking up new statements may reflect the fact that the problem is a long-standing one, so it is *obviously* bad, terrible, disgraceful, or whatever, and it is hard to see it in any other way. But our difficulty also arises from the fact that our beliefs and attitudes are ingrained. Check this out by using the model on somebody else's problem. You may well find it easier to come up with alternative points of view than when you apply it to your own problems.

As with the Sleight of Mouth, using this model still needs creative, lateral thought. At some point you have to *think* about the issues. Often the more stupid or ridiculous a point of view, the more chance there will be of it unlocking a problem. After all, if the solution was logical and sensible you would probably have solved it by now. Humour and the bizarre can do wonders to disturb long-standing mindsets.

REVERSAL

Each of these techniques approaches a problem from different angles, sometimes changing the point of view very slightly to achieve the new insight. One of the difficulties of creative approaches to problem-solving is knowing where to start. If you have a well prescribed method you can do something, but how do you move out of mindsets which dominate your thinking? The previous techniques do just that, of course, giving some structure and analysis as a catalyst to the non-analytical, non-structured creative process.

An even simpler method is to go in the opposite way from which you are going, to completely *reverse* your thinking. A so-called provocation technique called Reversal reverses the problem statement completely. So, for instance, 'We are short of skilled IT [information technology] people' would be

reversed to something like 'We have plenty of skilled IT
people.' From the reversal, issues are then raised consequent
upon the new 'truth'. In this case the issues might be:

- Given adequate people resources in IT, what developments
  might we wish to pursue?
- How did we achieve this staff position in the face of compe-
  tition?
- Are these people employees or subcontractors?
- Can we sell on their skills at a profit?
- What training or job benefits have brought about this
  position?

And so on. Each issue can be explored creatively, and you will
need to imagine what it would actually be like in the reversed
situation, just as a child can be somebody else or enter a new
world of make-believe. For example, if it were possible to on-
sell staff, paying a premium wage or contract rate might solve
the supply and demand problem, whilst ensuring continuity of
resources for in-house work and a potential profit centre; that
is, turning a problem into an opportunity. Any new problem
confronted along the line, such as finance or implementing an
idea, can be subject to the same reversal treatment.
Alternatively, the Sleight of Mouth and Points of View models
can be applied. Long-standing problems and company issues
have usually been the focus of lots of thought over a period,
and no doubt plenty of ideas have already been raised and
discounted. Building in the ultimate radical thinking – a
complete reversal of everything you know and believe about an
issue – will make a provocative impact on your thinking.

You don't need to split hairs on what constitutes a full
reversal. A group of managers may reverse a problem in
different ways. That is not the point; the point is to break out
of existing thinking patterns and to get started. The technique
is provocative rather than prescriptive, and if it sets the mind
working, it is doing its job.

Reversing a SWOT analysis

As a manager you may have used the popular SWOT
(strengths, weaknesses, opportunities, threats) analysis, which
is useful for strategic thinking and any sort of rethink at a

corporate, group or personal level. In the case of this conventional problem-solving tool, each item – whether a strength or weakness, opportunity or threat – is amenable to reversal. If you are familiar with using SWOTS you will know that in practice a threat, such as an interest rate change or currency movement, may also be a potential opportunity. The reversal technique ensures that in every case you turn the issue on its head. The trouble with any conventional, logical problem-solving technique is that any second-rate competitor can use the same devices, even doing a 'competitor SWOT' in respect of your company to help get competitive edge. This is exacerbated when systems are computerised, such as in the case of automatic stock market buy and sell signals, which can become sinisterly self-fulfilling.

Creative problem-solving taps into the limitless possibilities, by definition unrecognised, which might provide a solution. Just as individual managers operate successfully with different styles and values, and individual customer tastes are so diverse and unpredictable, so there is room for all sorts of creativity and innovation, allowing competing firms to grow on a win-win basis. Try applying the reversal technique to an existing SWOT analysis if you have done one recently. Alternatively apply it to your top half-dozen intractable but important problems or issues, whether work-related or personal.

Convenient business appraisal frames

Typically SWOT analyses can be fitted into a familiar structure such as:

- organisational
- environmental
- economic
- social
- political
- political (company, department)
- technical
- legal and regulatory
- personal
- ethical

and so on. These are convenient broad frames of reference,

and can certainly trigger the mind to produce long lists for your SWOT analysis. But these are unlikely to be very creative, as such a form of classification is not provocative, being logical and *convergent*, rather than radical, or lateral and *divergent*. The SWOT reversal is a good example of combining orthodox problem-solving or opportunity-generating techniques with creative reframing.

Rethinking priorities

The reversal idea need not be confined to reversing a written or spoken problem statement. It can be used in conjunction with more conventional left-brain approaches in a novel way. For example, you may decide to list the many factors that go to make up the problem – all the issues that will have to be given consideration. Put these in order of importance, just as you might prioritise your daily list of tasks. Now reverse the list, giving attention to the least important factors first. This will seem strange and uncomfortable, because your personal mental map *knows* what is important and unimportant.

The chances are that by sticking to your instinctive ways to analyse you will come up with either the same solutions (which in this case must be no good, or you wouldn't really have a problem in the first place) or the same blank wall. Of course your limited map might not even include the factor that turns out to be important, so you need to be as exhaustive as possible when listing the factors, even though you would normally give some of them precious little attention. This is a case where group input will reduce this tendency to be blinkered. But even in group work there is still value in the reversal, as often managers in an organisation, conditioned by its history and culture, or fellow professionals such as accountants or sales-people with similar training and functional rules, tend to adopt the same thinking patterns.

TYPES OF PROBLEM

There are other ways to approach problem-solving. Edward de Bono, for instance refers to three types of problem.

1. *The road is blocked*

   The first is where you know where you want to be, or what you want to achieve, but your path is blocked. The obstacle may be a shortage of resources, lack of some technology, or a 'people' issue, perhaps. Once your problem is solved, and the road is clear, you proceed to where you want to be.

2. *You run out of road*

   The second type of problem is where you exhaust all possibilities, and in effect run out of road. You may need more information, for instance, about market trends, technology changes, government policy and so on. Although your obstacle is not specific, at least you can proceed to get more information which may eventually provide the key so that you can move forward.

3. *You miss the turning*

   The third type is the most difficult. You don't know what the problem is. This is the case, for instance when you think everything is fine but realise when it is too late that you missed an opportunity. It's like going past a concealed side road without knowing it. The problem is only revealed later when you find, for instance, that a competitor spotted the side road and has beaten you. Not being able to recognise opportunities, or threats, is the problem.

The first of these three types of problem lends itself to conventional problem-solving techniques which require that you know what your problem is sufficiently to analyse it. In the second case you will rely a lot more on judgement, not knowing the sort of information that might be relevant, how to assess its reliability, and when to stop getting more of it and making a decision. The third case really needs an intuitive approach that will detect the smallest signs of opportunities that might help you in your ultimate outcome or mission. Analytical problem-solving approaches – which apply to just about all such management techniques – are no good if you don't know what to analyse.

Adequate or best solution?

Reframing can be applied to each type of problem. Even a clearly defined problem may defy solution, and different thinking is required. A lateral approach does not assume, in any event, that there is just *one* solution – the *best* solution, rather than an adequate one, is the aim. In the second case, the more uncertain you are of the facts, the more the issues have to be seen in a holistic way so that you don't waste time tackling the wrong problems or amassing the wrong data. In the third case the answer is not in techniques and models, so much as adopting a more creative way of thinking all the time, and this comes with an understanding of the presuppositions and thinking stages we have discussed, and *practice* in reframing any situation you meet. Success in opportunity search is also linked with strong outcomes, upon which the necessary unconscious associations are based. If you are watching out for a side road because your outcome may depend on it (it could be a better, quicker way to get to where you want to be) you are more likely to spot it. If your goal is to open up Far East markets, or to build a study in the loft, you will be more likely to spot helpful signals from newspapers, conversations and otherwise unlikely sources. In order to spot problems that don't make themselves known, you need to trust your right brain to help you achieve your outcomes cybernetically.

18

Problems and Opportunities

SOME MANAGERS like to differentiate between problems and opportunities. Marketing and salespeople and seasoned positive thinkers dislike the very term 'problem', preferring to express everything as an opportunity. In one sense this is part of the way we perceive things differently – the 'half full or half empty glass' idea – and forms part of the different macro strategies we met earlier. An understanding of reframing principles makes the distinction somewhat semantic, as all we do in this and every situation is put things into some frame or other – in this case a 'problem' frame or an 'opportunity' frame. As long as an opportunity remains unrealised, however, it constitutes a problem, whatever language we use. And implicit in every problem is a solution, and the opportunity to find it. So, for better or worse, and to stay on what is familiar territory for most managers as professional problem-solvers, I refer to problem-solving.

Problem-solving and problem-finding

From a pragmatic management point of view it may be better to distinguish between problem-*solving* and problem-*finding*. The first is much easier than the second, as we have something to react to – something we can *do*. It is characteristic of reactive management generally, which is widespread. *Projective* thinking, on the other hand, sees problems that we have not been made aware of, the third type described earlier, which are usually the sort that create the most damage, but whose solution can offer the biggest payback.

The complacency that seems to affect some highly successful corporations, as smaller companies gain the technological and marketing edge, illustrates this distinction. It's what you have not foreseen, or what does not appear as an identifiable obstacle, that will turn out to be the biggest problem. The expression 'a victim of your own success' also relates to the dangers of not being in a continuous problem-finding mode. Call it opportunity search, if you wish, but one way or another we need to get out of a linear mode, into projective thinking that excludes no opportunity and no problem either. De Bono's definitions of both terms are at the same time slick and thought-provoking: a problem is something you want to do but cannot; an opportunity is something you do not yet know you want to do – and can. Reframing can help in both cases.

Bicameral thinking

Managers need to have skills in what are loosely left- and right-brain approaches. Respective skills will come into their own at different times in the life of an organisation, depending on the prevailing circumstances, as well as the strategy. In a time of retrenchment and cost-cutting a lot of analysis and focused thinking will be needed. In an expansion mode, involving perhaps acquisitions and product diversification, with no historical base from which to project, a more creative, open approach is needed. The need for balance, however, or bicameral thinking, which I have already stressed, is illustrated in the familiar case of cost-cutting for efficiency. Initially, a simple analysis will usually result in savings. However, when trying to find further successive savings you need to be much more creative. Similarly, a rational, systematic approach to acquisitions or market opportunities may work if an existing product/market strategy is being followed. But more creative thinking is needed when you are looking to change your strategy into new product and markets. The biggest impact, however, is made when creative reframing is applied at every stage and *in conjunction* with rigorous analytical techniques, as in the case of reversed SWOT analysis.

SUSPENDING JUDGEMENT

The approaches we have considered so far may mean that you have to suspend judgement. In the case of reversal, in particular, managers sometimes react strongly against wasting time on pursuing ideas which seem to them patent nonsense. This is symptomatic of a strong left brain dominance among managers and professionally trained people, as well as a lack of understanding of the process of quality thinking, including the role of the subconscious. Ironically, although we are all only too aware of the importance of other people suspending judgement when we are trying to get across a proposal to someone who is sceptical, we find it hard to do it ourselves. This is because of the feeling of 'rightness' of our own mind patterns. And the more entrenched these are, the more difficult it is to suspend judgement. But the benefits of a creative approach are too fundamental to be missed. So-called sound judgement will block an idea, in favour of an alternative *adequate* solution, when there is a possibility of a *better* solution. More pragmatically, the need to be always right means we become afraid of making mistakes – even though most successful managers will usually attribute their very success to the mistakes they have learned from. And even an incorrect idea might result in solving some other problem.

Suspending judgement doesn't mean you abandon it, but that you *delay* it, to allow time for lateral choices. As we saw in the thinking stages, judgement, sometimes involving a period of incubation, is usually considered a right-brain function, rather than a mechanical, analytical process, and is needed in every aspect of a problem or task. For example, judgements have to be made:

- as to whether the information or 'facts' you have are relevant to the problem;
- about when, and in what way, to communicate an idea to others;
- on an idea coming from someone else;
- about the resources needed, or benefits that might accrue from one course of action or another;
- in terms of assumptions;
- about people involved, such as who might be best to fulfil a

task, or how a person might react;
- about timescale;
- about long-term effects;
and so on.

Although you can only quantify the importance of suspending judgement with the benefit of hindsight on a particular problem you have faced, it does make a lot of sense:

- an idea might survive longer and stimulate more ideas, any of which could be a winner;
- other people are in turn more inclined to suspend their judgement, and so there is reciprocal benefit;
- changing circumstances might make ideas that would otherwise have been quashed useful on a different timescale;
- the skill and habit of suspending judgement makes for many more personal choices, and better rather than merely adequate outcomes.

The various NLP reframing models and techniques will help us to suspend judgement when naturally we tend to follow our own comfortable maps of what is 'good', 'right', or 'reasonable'.

REFRAMING APPLIED TO CONVENTIONAL PROBLEM-SOLVING

There are a number of problem-solving approaches and techniques which you may be familiar with. I have already referred to the different stages in the problem definition and decision process, and applied some NLP ideas to that model. Additional benefit can also be got from individual techniques by adding more creativity. I mentioned, for example, applying the reversal provocation technique to a SWOT analysis. In this section I will give further examples.

Force field analysis

This is not the place to describe common analytical problem-solving techniques, but, in a nutshell, force field analysis identifies the positive and negative forces at work in any situation. For instance, there are some things that make meetings productive and worthwhile, and there are other things that make them ineffective. The relative strengths of these positive and negative forces will determine whether the meeting is effective or not. By identifying the 'forces', or factors at work, a better idea of the problem will be attained. A compromise or trade-off solution, for instance, may become apparent, or specific factors, such as a weak chairperson or inconvenient timing of the meeting, can be tackled. In NLP terms these are just different frames or points of view on the problem. In this case two basic frames are used – positive and negative, which are akin to the important empowering and disempowering distinction NLP applies to behaviour in relation to outcomes.

Weighting forces

At a simple level, the analysis will list positive and negative forces. Using the example just quoted, have two columns headed 'What makes meetings productive and effective?' and 'What makes meetings unproductive and ineffective?' For the technique to be useful, however, you need to be as specific as possible. Avoid nominalisations such as 'communication' or 'conflict', and stick to specifics – preferably behaviour – like 'agenda not distributed in time' or 'starting an hour before finishing time'. Go back to the tests of an outcome to get back to basics.

The force field tool will be more effective if the factors are *weighted*. One negative force (say, the person chairing the meeting), for instance, might outweigh a whole list of positive forces, or vice versa. Stronger forces can therefore be given more attention, either putting your mind to eliminating them, or coming up with strong enough counter-forces.

What is crucial to overall effectiveness is likely to be a matter of judgement, of course. And, just as important, the list itself usually turns out be highly subjective – different people identify different factors at play, especially when experienced, articulate people are involved. Generating force field lists, therefore, needs creativity and insight; applying weighting to give real meaning requires even more.

The earlier reframing techniques can be applied to any problem and the positive and negative aspects are covered in most models. The force field model simply highlights the effect of these forces acting against each other, and the net result which determines the outcome. The many angles identified through the other reframing techniques will also give insight into the importance of each factor, or relevant weighting.

Problem recognition techniques

Several techniques address the problem-finding, or problem-recognition part of the problem-solving process. Data-gathering, 'symptom' identification, research methodology, and group brainstorming, for instance, may be involved. Conventional techniques major on hard data – statistics, results, objectives, trends, performance levels, and suchlike. Soft data may be concerned with feelings, beliefs, opinions, attitudes, personalities, individual behaviour, intuition, 'gut feelings', reactions and so on. The thinking stages we met earlier illustrate this. The danger for logical thinking managers is to deny or play down soft data and the subjective aspects of a problem. In practice, however, these aspects usually represent the lion's share of the issues involved – the under-water part of the iceberg – so need to have our best attention. Divergent or creative approaches therefore tend to give better returns than more analytical techniques, which often involve going over the same logical ground again and again.

Here are some approaches to problem recognition.

Symptoms

Taking a product, market, department or any 'chunk' of the organisation, list *symptoms*, or known issues or factors. For a product, for instance, you might list:

- sales fall-off over last three months
- component supply bottlenecks
- low morale in plant
- effect of new product launches
- recurring plant maintenance snags
- new competitor just launching.

These can be classified as requiring hard or soft data to enable the problems to be defined. Some symptoms, such as sales figures or inventory levels, will have hard supportive data, while other symptoms will involve subjective judgements, whether about people, the effect of technology, or what might happen in the future. But in each case problems are likely to be identified from the list of symptoms, and they can then be better defined (labelled), and so become amenable to the various problem-solving approaches we have covered.

Overall, product X might not be a problem, and may have as many positive symptoms as negative ones. The important thing is not to kid yourself – problems must be found before they find you, and nipped in the bud. The earlier you find a problem, the more chance there will be of turning it into an opportunity. The longer you leave it the more chance it will have of becoming a symptom, or a 'compound' problem, the root cause of which is hard to identify. Behind each symptom you should be able to identify one or more problems you can address specifically.

Data collection

Various research methods are available to enable us to investigate issues and problems in a proactive rather than reactive way. For example, there are questionnaires, interviews, production, quality and financial statistics, attitude and other surveys, work sampling, focus groups, etc. As with a symptom analysis, these are more than likely to identify problems which can then be subjected to reframing techniques. They will also comprise hard and soft data, and thus demand imagination and judgement. As with all problem-finding, opportunities will arise if you adopt the right frame of mind.

Reframing

The reframing approaches we have met are also useful for problem recognition. Usually they throw up plenty of new issues, so there will be no shortage of pertinent problems or opportunities to address as a spin-off of the process. The new problem that a reframe reveals may well be the critical factor, or root cause. So apply reframing thinking to any conventional technique as a problem-finding tool.

More conservative managers are not at all comfortable with changing their frames of reference, because of the new realities this uncovers. They are happier to stick with visible symptoms that may conceal several fundamental problems, and even in this case often discount 'soft' factors that cannot be quantified. More than anything, reframing exposes our own limited perceptions.

Brainstorming

This is probably the best-known example of creative problem-solving, having been around for many years, and can also be used for problem-recognition. Again, I will not describe the basics which are well covered elsewhere. Because it is a familiar tool of creative thinking which many managers will have used before, I will comment on it more specifically in relation to some of the principles we have already discussed.

More effective brainstorming

Assuming for present purposes that the group brainstorming is well facilitated, and ideas are not suppressed or subjected to criticism or evaluation, there are still a few pitfalls to be aware of. I have already stressed that much of NLP applies particularly at a personal level, and does not necessarily relate to an organisation, or group. We have already seen, moreover, that many problems are in any event to do with interpersonal communication, and wherever this is the case, there is potential for problems over and above the ones you set out to solve. For instance, even in a group brainstorming for the purpose of generating new ideas, there will be attitudes, preconceptions, egos, office politics, and probably point-scoring, just as in a meeting or any other work or social gathering. All this detracts from the openness needed for any creative process and limits group processes of any kind. Some chief executives are sceptical about brainstorming sessions as typically run, sometimes at outside expensive venues to give the right creative atmosphere. Peer pressure and hierarchical relationships also tend to make the contributions a little lopsided. One or two people take up the 'airtime', regardless of the quality of their input. Paradoxically, in terms of individual creativity, the less vocal members could probably think of dozens of ideas either on their own or perhaps in after-work discussion with another colleague. So group brainstorming can be very inefficient if the purpose is to generate plenty of creativity; 'diminishing returns' tend to apply, both as numbers increase, and as the time spent extends.

There may also be the desire to have tangible outputs from the session, even though in the nature of brainstorming and other creativity techniques no such guarantees can be given. More specifically, in the attempt to come up with lateral, off-the-wall ideas, there may be a lack of focus.

Freewheeling focus

Paradoxically, what is ostensibly a freewheeling process needs to focus:

- on the purpose or outcome (outcome frame), however free and easy the approach, whether it is to unblock a problem, identify issues, exploit an opportunity, or whatever;
- on the process (process frame), avoiding both long silences, personal hobby horses, rank etc.

As far as the outcome is concerned, refer back to the criteria for a well-formed outcome. Even an outcome like '20 new ideas in half an hour, addressing X subject, with at least two suggestions from each member' will meet the main criteria, and the session is likely to be productive.

As far as the process is concerned, good facilitation is needed, and it should follow the standard rules ('No judgement, evaluation, criticism, etc.') for brainstorming sessions.

Unless there is outcome and process focus, creativity is likely to be dissipated. The big danger is that these group processes take on a life of their own, complete with structure and entrenched mindsets.

Combining reframing techniques

Some structure and focus can also be got by using some of the earlier reframing techniques in combination with group brainstorming. Sleight of Mouth, Points of View, or reversal provocation techniques are models that stimulate maximum creativity, and can be used in a group setting, although the risks increase and good facilitation is needed. SWOT and force field analysis are neater analytical tools but you may slip into the trap of taking a historical, linear or rational point of view. The Sleight of Mouth model works particularly well in a small group, as each member can take a turn in giving a response based on the various points of view. Not only is every person involved, incorporating all the different backgrounds and personal experience, but they can rotate the 'points of view' so that each person is required to think from each perspective. It is sometimes advisable for the problem holder to leave his or her colleagues to provide questions and responses, so that existing expertise and 'wisdom' is not allowed to get in the way. He will have plenty of chances to get involved in evaluation and eventual implementation, and can reciprocate by changing positions when somebody else's problem is addressed. When using these techniques in a group, the brainstorming requires creativity for response questions, and freedom from summary critical judgement.

Key word analysis

Different people attach different meanings to words, and this can make problem-solving much more difficult than it need be, while in some cases it is the cause of the problem in the first place. Although the problems created in this way are semantic, they can have the same effect as a resources or technological problem. The analysis involves selecting the words that seem to cause the problem (such as 'quality', 'communication', 'on target', 'delegate', 'defects', or 'acceptable'. Note that these are likely to be nominalisations, such as we met in the Meta Model, rather than sensory-friendly words such as 'Fred', 'aluminium', or 'plastic spacers'.

In key word analysis the key words are defined specifically in as many ways as possible, then one meaning is selected that everyone agrees upon, or an offending word is replaced. The agreed word is used in the 'label', or specific problem statement, which then becomes the agreed understanding of the problem.

Sometimes this process seems to takes you backward, as new problems come out of the woodwork, different issues are identified, and personal factors are brought into the open. But in the long term this is an important part of the problem-solving process. Sometimes the different word definitions reflect different functional biases, sometimes level of seniority and knowledge of the issues, individual role, or personal close involvement with the problem. Words like 'output', 'quality', or 'efficiency' might conjure share prices in the mind of the chairman, bottom line profits in the mind of the accountant, new markets or sales to the marketing people, and 'less than one per cent rejects' to the quality or manufacturing manager.

Using the Meta Model

This is a simple but effective tool. Mutually defining the key words allows strong functional or parochial viewpoints to be resolved at an early stage. When it comes to exorcising semantics, however, the Meta Model is in a different league. As well as the nominalisations which typically turn out to be problematical, universal quantifiers will similarly have to be questioned. 'X department is *never* on time', or 'Joe *always* does so and so' will have to be qualified and a deeper meaning identified. Comparisons such as 'better' or 'worse', or implied comparisons inside or outside the company, will also fail to get through the Meta Model questioning process. So you have a powerful tool that has been used successfully to clarify imprecise statements in any communication, including problem definition. Faulty language patterns that are not immediately identified by words (and which might be missed in a key word analysis), such as cause and effect, should be caught in the Meta Model net. In any event you can apply Meta Model questions to problems that arise from the labelled problems the key word analysis throws up.

Problem-cause analysis

This technique attempts to arrive at the true problem defin-ition, in terms of the source or cause of the symptom or apparent problem. Often the source of the problem is control-lable and solvable – and quite simple – so it is worth the effort of getting at its root. As we have seen already, the symptoms of a problem may just be the visible part of an iceberg, and the true problem is hidden. Moreover, what is invisible may include a number of problems which have not been identified and addressed. Waiting to be identified, and usually the key to the solution, the root cause is what has been described as the 'limiting factor'.

Identifying the 'limiting factor'

For example, a symptom may be described as 'poor staff morale'. Problem-cause analysis tries to identify the factors that are causing this, such as low pay, poor working conditions, lack of training, declining market for the product, limited car parking, remote management, fears of plant closure, and so on. It may turn out that 'fear of plant closure' is the major contributory factor, or 'limiting factor', and that this has resulted from rumours started somewhere inside the company, but which have no basis. Usually the root cause, when finally identified, is readily solvable. If it is not, it may be that you have not quite arrived at the limiting factor, or cause of the problem.

In the above case, specific measures can be taken to communicate the truth about the future of the plant. If, on the other hand, lack of training turns out to be the cause, resources can be put in and no doubt a good return would be obtained in the form of higher morale and consequent output improvement. Even 'poor management' might relate to one or a couple of people, or just one aspect of management or communication. The further back you get to the cause, the more specific and treatable the problem is likely to be. That does not mean that solutions are easy. In fact treating the real problem may be more distasteful or demanding than tackling the other contributing factors or symptoms – but now you have a better understanding, and you have a choice.

As it happens, root problems have often been caused by attempted solutions to other perceived problems in the past. For instance, a pep talk to correct falling output, including implicit threats to long-term security, might well have triggered rumours about closure of the plant. Finding the cause is like finding the key to unlock a door, or the keystone to an arch in a building. Identify the key and you unlock the problem; remove the keystone and, like a structure without support, the rest of the related problems collapse.

The 'aha' moment

Although this is a standard analytical technique, to be effective you need to exercise a lot of creativity. The final 'aha' moment, when you identify what is really causing the problem is more like an insight or a eureka than the sequential result of any logical process. One of the skills you need is to distinguish between cause and effect, working backwards until you get to the offending source of a problem. This technique can be used in conjunction with several others. For instance, any of the provocation techniques you have met will throw light on what might be an over-familiar problem. One of the factors in a force field analysis might similarly identify a root cause. Other techniques that might help are chronological analysis, and repetitive why? analysis.

Chronological analysis

From the problem-cause analysis it soon becomes apparent that one problem causes another, and that a sequential or chronological path can be traced. The skill is to trace backwards from your present problem to see how you got to where you are, thus finding the source problem. As I have just described, often a quick-fix solution only produces more problems, and other side-effects as well. Over the months, people forget the reasons why things were done, and unfortunately we don't often learn the lessons we should when experience stares us in the face. Chronological analysis starts with the present time and examines major symptoms or causes, and what led to them, and so on backwards in time. The end result is the same as in the problem-cause analysis, except that your 'frame' is chronological. Although the process is a systematic one, connections between cause and effect are usually far from obvious or even logical. So the right-brain power of association will need to be brought into play, and this comes less by conscious trying than by being in a receptive or freewheeling frame of mind.

Repetitive 'Why?' analysis

This is a similar technique. Many techniques, including NLP ones, generate scores of possible contributory causes and you may be left more confused than when you started. Choices are fine, but you have to do something with them. What you are after is the 'aha' that lets you know you have hit on the critical cause. This technique starts with the present problem statement and applies the sort of phrase '. . .which was caused by' repeatedly. For example:

'Two important orders were lost' which was caused by
'Delays in following up simple queries' which were caused by
'The filing system is almost out of control' which was caused by
'Sarah going on leave' which was caused by . . .

and so on.

Not only does the process take you nearer and nearer to the real cause of a problem, but usually there is a 'ring of truth' when you go the next step back and you know you have cracked it. This 'rightness' does not sound rational, and perhaps isn't. The unconscious right brain is doing its job again, and communicating its findings to the conscious left side. But typically you will feel you have got at the root problem; the insight will often explain a lot of other things that did not make sense before. Rather like the final missing piece of a jigsaw puzzle, there is a finality about it – you get the whole picture; and a further practical test is that you are more than likely to get agreement in a group as to the true nature of the problem. Another characteristic of a root problem we have already met is that it tends to be quite specific and solvable – although you may have to take decisive action to bring it about.

Reframing is a way of thinking – perhaps even a way of life. In one sense you don't do it by techniques, models or systems. The right brain is the anarchic side of our thinking and it revels in turning systems upside down, reinventing perfectly respectable models, and taking short cuts in problem-solving that should not be allowed. But provided we recognise and respect this awesome but often latent creativity, there are certainly useful ways of stimulating and harnessing brainpower which is there for the using. Nor does our access to the more mystical, unconscious side of the mind mean we have to abandon logic, rationale and our love as managers for analysis. It's a partnership. Some jobs that you do need high conscious concentration, while at other times you need to let a matter go below the surface, and maybe sleep on it for a while. Each different way of thinking serves you very well, but together, there is an almost godlike potential for creating a different future.

* * *

You have hardly begun to tap your true potential as a manager – as a person. The simple, but universally useful, presuppositions of NLP can form the basis of a whole new way of thinking. Once the mystique is removed from excellent behaviour, and the thought processes that underlie it, the real barriers – barriers in the mind – are there to be overcome one by one. Once we can tap into our own experiences of mastery, and use them in other areas of life, our achievements will become more consistent and success will become natural and self-generating. Where resolution and willpower have failed, new habits of unconscious competence will start to account for more of our successes.

With all this comes a new self-awareness and personal responsibility. NLP, we saw, applies the important ecology check to all our outcomes. Its approach is *holistic*, both in tapping the unconscious as well as the conscious mind, and also in reframing experience to create many more choices. As we have seen in this final part, there are plenty of techniques you can use to reframe problems and events, whether at work or in your personal life. And if there are attitudes and beliefs you need to change first, you now have the tools to change them.

A few empowering personal beliefs, and a willingness to accept and apply the simple presuppositions of NLP, will then multiply the power of the techniques and models. With a little practice, the communication skills you have met, both verbal and non-verbal, the personal strategies for competence and mastery, and the problem-solving reframing tools we have just described, will become an integral part of your thinking and behaviour as a manager. Most of all, your personal map of reality will be richer and more useful. Many people find that the *process* of learning, changing, and seeing things differently – as well as the outcomes they achieve – brings its own pleasure. The journey, as well as the destination takes on a new meaning. Whatever your own desired outcomes, NLP provides the people-friendly technology for you to achieve them.

◀ GLOSSARY ▶

Associated   Seeing an experience as if through your own eyes.

Chunking   Going down or up a level, to see a situation in more detail or from a wider perspective respectively.

Complex equivalence   Two statements that are meant to mean the same thing (e.g. 'she walked past me, she is annoyed').

Content Reframing   Focusing on another part or aspect of a statement or experience to give it a different meaning. (What else could this mean?).

Context Reframing   Changing the context of a statement or experience to give it a different meaning. (In what other context would this be appropriate?).

Dissociated   Seeing an experience as if through someone else's eyes – from outside yourself.

Downtime   The state when your attention is on your own inner thoughts, e.g. when preoccupied or daydreaming.

Ecology   Used in NLP as the relationship between the various thoughts and behaviours of an individual, including their different outcomes.

First Position   Perceiving the world from your own point of view, rather than as someone else sees things (see also second and third positions).

Future Pacing   Mentally rehearsing a future outcome to help bring it about.

Meta Model   A model that identifies imprecise language patterns and gives questions and responses to clarify or challenge them.

Mirroring   Matching other people's behaviour to bring about rapport.

Mismatching   Adopting different behaviour patterns, thus breaking rapport (e.g. to end a conversation).

Modal Operator of Necessity   A Meta Model term that includes rules involving 'should', 'ought', etc.

Neurological levels   Different levels of experience: environment, behaviour, capability, belief, identity.

Perceptual Positions   Different viewpoints as in first, second and third perceptual positions.

Predicates   Words expressing the use of a representational system, e.g. 'It sounds OK'.

Presuppositions   Statements that have to be taken for granted for a communication to make sense.

Reframing   Changing the frame of reference round a statement or experience to give it another meaning.

Representation System   How we code sensory information internally, using vision, hearing, feelings, taste and smell.

Second position   Seeing things from another person's point of view (see also first and third positions).

Strategy   A sequence of thought and behaviour that brings about a certain outcome.

Submodality   The qualities and characteristics of our representation systems, e.g. the size and brightness of an internal image.

Third Position   The perspective of a detached outside observer (see also first position and second position).

Timeline   The way we represent time, storing pictures of our past, present and future.

Universal Quantifiers   A Meta Model language term that includes words such as 'every', 'all' and 'never'.

Uptime   A state of focused attention, where the senses are used outwardly rather than inwardly.

◄ FURTHER READING ►

Frogs into Princes, Richard Bandler and John Grinder, Real People Press (1979).

Heart of the Mind, Connirae Andreas and Steve Andreas, Real People Press (1989).

Introducing Neuro-Linguistic Programming, Joseph O'Connor and John Seymour, HarperCollins (1990).

NLP: The New Art and Science of Getting What You Want, Dr Harry Alder, Piatkus (1994).

NLP: The New Technology of Achievement, Steve Andreas and Charles Faulkner (Editors), *NLP Comprehensive* (1994).

Psychocybernetics, Maxwell Maltz, Simon and Schuster (1960).

Reframing, Richard Bandler and John Grinder, Real People Press (1982).

Unlimited Power, Anthony Robbins, Simon and Schuster (1986).

Using Your Brain for a Change, Richard Bandler, Real People Press (1985).

◄ INDEX ►

Piatkus Business Books

Piatkus Business Books have been created for people who need expert knowledge readily available in a clear and easy-to-follow format. All the books are written by specialists in their field. They will help you improve your skills quickly and effortlessly in the workplace and on a personal level.

Titles include:

General Management and Business Skills
Be Your Own PR Expert: the complete guide to publicity and public relations Bill Penn
Complete Conference Organiser's Handbook, The Robin O'Connor
Complete Time Management System, The Christian H. Godefroy and John Clark
Confident Decision Making J. Edward Russo and Paul J. H. Schoemaker
Corporate Culture Charles Hampden-Turner
Energy Factor, The: how to motivate your workforce Art McNeil
Firing On All Cylinders: the quality management system for high-powered corporate performance Jim Clemmer with Barry Sheehy
How to Implement Change in Your Company John Spencer and Adrian Pruss
Influential Manager, The: How to develop a powerful management style Lee Bryce
Influential Woman, The: How to achieve success in your career – and still enjoy your personal life Lee Bryce
Lure the Tiger Out of the Mountains: timeless tactics from the East for today's successful manager Gao Yuan
Managing For Performance Alasdair White
Managing Your Team John Spencer and Adrian Pruss
Problem Solving Techniques That Really Work Malcolm Bird
Right Brain Time Manager, The Dr Harry Alder
Seven Cultures of Capitalism, The: value systems for creating wealth in Britain, the United States, Germany, France, Japan, Sweden and the Netherlands Charles Hampden-Turner and Fons Trompenaars
Smart Questions for Successful Managers Dorothy Leeds
Think Like A Leader Dr Harry Alder

Personnel and People Skills
Best Person for the Job, The Malcolm Bird

Dealing with Difficult People Roberta Cava
Problem Employees: how to improve their behaviour and their performance Peter Wylie and Mardy Grothe
Psychological Testing for Managers Dr Stephanie Jones
Tao of Negotiation: How to resolve conflict in all areas of your life Joel Edelman and Mary Beth Crain

Financial Planning
Better Money Management Marie Jennings
Great Boom Ahead, The Harry Dent
How to Choose Stockmarket Winners Raymond Caley
Perfectly Legal Tax Loopholes Stephen Courtney
Practical Fundraising For Individuals And Small Groups David Wragg

Small Business
How to Earn Money from Your Personal Computer Polly Bird
How to Run a Part-Time Business Barrie Hawkins
Making Money From Your Home Hazel Evans
Marketing On A Tight Budget Patrick Forsyth
Profit Through the Post: How to set up and run a successful mail order business Alison Cork

Motivational
Play to Your Strengths O. Clifton and Paula Nelson
Super Success Philip Holden
Winning Edge, The Charles Templeton

Self-Improvement
Brain Power: the 12-week mental training programme Marilyn vos Savant and Leonore Fleischer
Creative Thinking Michael LeBoeuf
Napoleon Hill's Keys To Success Matthew Sartwell (ed.)
Napoleon Hill's Unlimited Success Matthew Sartwell (ed.)
NLP: The New Art and Science of Getting What You Want Dr Harry Alder
Personal Growth Handbook, The Liz Hodgkinson
Personal Power Philippa Davies
Quantum Learning: unleash the genius within you Bobbi DePorter with Mike Hernacki
Right Brain Manager, The: how to use the power of your mind to achieve personal and professional success Dr Harry Alder
10-Minute Time And Stress Management Dr David Lewis
Three Minute Meditator, The David Harp with Nina Feldman
Total Confidence Philippa Davies

For a free brochure with further information on our complete range of business titles, please write to:

Piatkus Books
Freepost 7 (WD 4505)
London W1E 4EZ

PIATKUS